ENCYCLOPAEDIA OF EMINENT THINKERS

VOLUME-XXVII: **GOPAL KRISHNA GOKHALE**

Volumes by the same author

The Political Thought of ***Veer Savarkar***
The Political Thought of ***M.A. Jinnah***
The Political Thought of ***Mohammad Iqbal***
The Political Thought of ***K.B. Hedgewar***
The Political Thought of ***M.S. Golwalkar***
The Political Thought of ***Lokmanya Bal Gangadhar Tilak***
The Political Thought of ***Pandit Deendayal Upadhyaya***
The Political Thought of ***Gopal Krishna Gokhale***
The Political Thought of ***Maulana Abul Kalam Azad***
The Political Thought of ***Sir Syed Ahmed Khan***

About the Author

Jai Narain Sharma (*b.* 1951) is Professor and Chairman of the Department of Gandhian Studies, Panjab University, Chandigarh. He is also Hon. Director of Gandhi Bhawan; member of Board of Studies, Nagpur University, Nagpur and Mahatma Gandhi Kashi Vidyapith, Varanasi; member of Research Degree Committee of the Department of Political Science, H.P. University, Shimla: General Secretary of Indian Soviety of Gandhian Studies; and member on the Presidium of the Alliance for Sarvodaya. He regularly writes for leading newspapers, and has published more than hundred research papers in professional journals of repute. Dr. Sharma has many books to his credit including *"Gandhi's View of Political Power", "Economics of Defence: A Study of SAARC Countries", "Economic Thought of Mahatma Gandhi", "Human Resource Management", "Alternative Economics: Economics of Mahatma Gandhi and Globalisation", "Power, Politics and Corruption: A Gandhian Solution"* and *"Research Methodology: The Discipline and its Dimensions.*

ENCYCLOPAEDIA OF EMINENT THINKERS

VOLUME-XXVII

THE POLITICAL THOUGHT OF GOPAL KRISHNA GOKHALE

Jai Narain Sharma
Professor
Department of Gandhian Studies
Panjab University
Chandigarh

CONCEPT PUBLISHING COMPANY, NEW DELHI-110 059

ISBN 13-978-81-7022-684-0 (Series) **ISBN 10-81-7022-684-8 (Series)**
ISBN 13-978-81-8069-635-0 (Vol. XXVII) **ISBN 10-81-8069-635-9 (Vol. XXVII)**

First Published 2010

Published and Printed by

Concept
Since 1974

Concept Publishing Company
Regd. Office:
A/15-16, Commercial Block, Mohan Garden
New Delhi-110059 (India)
Phones : 25351460, 25351794, *Fax* : 091-11-25357109
Email : publishing@conceptpub.com,
Website: www.conceptpub.com

Editorial Office:
H-13, Bali Nagar, New Delhi-110 015, India.

Cataloging in Publication Data-- *Courtesy:* D.K. Agencies (P) Ltd. docinfo@dkagencies.com

Encyclopaedia of eminent thinkers.
v. 26-30 cm. -- (Gandhian studies and peace research series ; 11)
Vols. 11- lack series statement.
In Indian context.
Includes bibliographical references. Includes indexes.
Contents: v. 26. The political thought of C.R. Das / Ashu Pasricha -- v. 27 The political thought of Gopal Krishna Gokhale / Jai Narain Sharma -- v. 28. The political thought of Lala Lajpat Rai / Ashu Pasricha -- v. 29. The political thought of Maulana Abul Kalam Azad / Jai Narain Sharma - v. 30. The political thought of Sir Pherozeshah Mehta / Ashu Pasricha.
ISBN 13: 9788170226840 (set) ISBN 10: 8170226848 (set)

1. Statesmen--India. 2. Political science--India. 3. India--Politics and government. I. Sharma, Jai Narain, 1951- II. Pasricha, Ashu, 1967- III. Series: Gandhian studies and peace research series ; 11.

DDC 954.035 22

DEDICATED
TO
THE SACRED MEMORYOF
MY
COLLEAGUE and FRIEND
(Late) SHRI L. M. SHARMA
(Department of Mass Communication)

PREFACE

Gopal Krishna Gokhale was born on May 9, 1866 and died on February 19, 1915. Lokmanya Tilak, writing an obituary article on Gokhale in the *Kesari* of 23rd February 1915, gave as its heading a verse from the *Mahabharata*: 'मुहूर्तं ज्वलितं श्रेयो न तु धूमायितं चिरम', which means, "Better burn out in a short-lived blaze than be smouldering for ever so long." The quotation was singularly appropriate to Gokhale's life and career. It was indeed a brilliant but shortlived blaze. A graduate at eighteen, Professor at twenty, Secretary of the Provincial Conference at twenty-two, Editor of a serious and influential journal like the Quarterly of the Poona Sarvajanik Sabha at twenty-four, Secretary of the National Congress at twenty-nine, an important witness before a Royal Commission—the Welby Commission—at thirty, Provincial Legislator at thirty-four, Imperial Legislator at thirty-six, President of the National Congress and founder of an Institution like the Servants of India Society at thirty-nine, member of a Royal Commission—the Islington Public Service Commission—at forty-six; what a brilliant career it was and how tragic that it should have been out at the early age of forty-eight!

Mahatma Gandhi, in his brochure, Gokhale—My Political Guru, observed:

> "It was a case of love at first sight, and it stood the severest strain in 1913. He seemed to me all I wanted as a political worker—pure as crystal, gentle as a lamb, brave as a lion, and chivalrous to a fault. It does not matter to me that he may not have been any of those things. It was enough for me that I could discover no fault in him to cavil at. He was and remains

One can easily imagine, after a reading of the Speeches and Writings of Gokhale, how the innate nobility of his nature, his dedication to the cause of freedom and prosperity for his countrymen, and above all the religious and humanistic Spirit in which he did all his public work produced deep impression on a kindred spirit. Gokhale enunciated in the Constitution of the Servants of India Society what he considered to be the requisites of a public worker in India in the following words:

> "Public life must be spiritualized. Love of country must so fill the heart that all else shall appear as of little moment by its side. A fervent patriotism which rejoices at every opportunity of sacrifice for the motherland, a dauntless heart which refuses to be turned back from its object by difficulty or danger, a deep faith in the purpose of Providence which nothing can shake—equipped with these, the worker must start on his mission and reverently seek the joy which comes of spending oneself in the service of one's country."

My work has benefited from the advice and suggestions of Professor R.N. Pal, former Pro-Vice Chancellor, Panjab University, Patiala, Dr. K.S. Bharti, Head, Department of Gandhian Thought, Nagpur University, Nagpur, Dr. A.D. Mishra, Deputy Director, National Gandhi Museum, New Delhi, Dr. R.P. Duvedi, Head, Department of Gandhian Thought, Mahatma Gandhi Kashi Vidyapeeth, Varanasi, Professor B.R. Dugar and Dr. Anil Dhar, Jain Vishwabharati Institute, Deemed University, Ladnun, Professor Raj Singh, Department of Sociology, H.A.U. Hissar, Professor Rakesh Dutta and Dr. (Ms) Meena Dutta, Department of Defence and Strategic Analysis, Panjab University, Chandigarh.

I am deeply indebted to my colleagues in the department—Dr. M.L. Sharma and Dr. Ashu Pasricha— who were good enough to read through a draft of the book and from whose many penetrating criticism and constructive suggestions I have benefited more than I can say.

There are many other teacher colleagues and students who

have contributed in so many ways and I express my thanks to them.

To my wife Rashmi, I owe the deepest debt for her emotional support, her unfailing encouragement and her undispensable contribution towards providing the environment in which I could complete this work.

Thanks are also due to my publisher Shri Ashok Kumar Mittal for the keen interest he has shown in this project.

Chandigarh **JAI NARAIN SHARMA**

Encyclopaedia of Eminent Thinkers Series

Vol. I. The Political Thought of Mahatma Gandhi/ *K.S. Bharti*
Vol. II. The Political Thought of Nehru/ *K.S. Bharti*
Vol. III. The Political Thought of Rabindra Nath Tagore/ *K.S. Bharti*
Vol. IV. The Political Thought of Radhakrishnan/ *K.S. Bharti*
Vol. V. The Political Thought of Vinoba/ *K.S. Bharti*
Vol. VI. The Political Thought of Aurobindo/ *K.S. Bharti*
Vol. VII. The Political Thought of Jayaprakash Narayan/ *K.S. Bharti*
Vol. VIII. The Political Thought of Vivekananda/ *K.S. Bharti*
Vol. IX. The Political Thought of Ambedkar/ *K.S. Bharti*
Vol. X. The Political Thought of M.N. Roy/ *K.S. Bharti*
Vol. XI. The Political Thought of Dadabhai Naoroji/ *Ashu Pasricha*
Vol. XII. The Political Thought of Veer Savarkar/ *Jai Narain Sharma*
Vol. XIII. The Political Thought of M.A. Jinnah/ *Jai Narain Sharma*
Vol. XIV. The Political Thought of Tej Bahadur Sapru/ *Ashu Pasricha*
Vol. XV. The Political Thought of C. Rajagopalachari/ *Ashu Pasricha*
Vol. XVI. The Political Thought of Subhas Chandra Bose/ *Ashu Pasricha*
Vol. XVII. The Political Thought of Mohammad Iqbal/ *Jai Narain Sharma*
Vol. XVIII. The Political Thought of K.B. Hedgewar/ *Jai Narain Sharma*
Vol. XIX. The Political Thought of Bhagat Singh/ *Ashu Pasricha*
Vol. XX. The Political Thought of M.S. Golwalkar/ *Jai Narain Sharma*
Vol. XXI. The Political Thought of Sir Syed Ahmed Khan/ *Jai Narain Sharma*
Vol. XXII. The Political Thought of Mahadev Govind Ranade/ *Ashu Pasricha*
Vol. XXIII. The Political Thought of Pandit Deendayal Upadhyaya/ *Jai Narain Sharma*
Vol. XXIV. The Political Thought of Lokmanya Bal Gangadhar Tilak/ *Jai Narain Sharma*
Vol. XXV. The Political Thought of Annie Besant/ *Ashu Pasricha*
Vol. XXVI. The Political Thought of C.R. Das/ *Ashu Pasricha*
Vol. XXVII. The Political Thought of Gopal Krishna Gokhale/ *Jai Narain Sharma*
Vol. XXVIII. The Political Thought of Lala Lajpat Rai/ *Ashu Pasricha*
Vol. XXIX. The Political Thought of Maulana Abul Kalam Azad/ *Jai Narain Sharma*
Vol. XXX. The Political Thought of Sir Pherozeshah Mehta/ *Ashu Pasricha*

CONTENTS

1

LIFE AND ACTIVITIES

Gokhale was born on May 9, 1866, at a village called Kotluk in Ratnagiri district of the old Bombay Presidency. The Gokhale family originally belonged to a village called Velaneshwar in that district. His forefathers moved to an adjoining village, Tamhapmala, obviously for economic reasons.

The family owned some landed property which was carefully managed. But the holdings in Ratnagiri district are not very fertile for food crops, nor large in acreage. It is a hilly district. Though the annual rainfall is more than 80 inches on an average, much of it drains to the sea, leaving little for cultivation during the rest of the year. A coastal district, Ratnagiri has enchanting scenery. It is a fruit growing area: mango, cocoanut, cashewnut and jack fruit abound.

Gokhale came from a middle class family which was somewhat well off. 'Waste not, want not' is generally the motto of the caste to which Gokhale belonged,[1] the Chitpavan Brahmins, much misrepresented by writers like Sir Valentine Chirol.[2] The Chitpavan Brahmins have certain distinctive characteristics. They are practical and ambitious, personable and industrious. By dint of these qualities, the Chitpavan Brahmins, although numbering but a few lakhs, have come to the forefront in many wafts of life. The Peshwas who ruled Maharashtra for over a hundred years were Chitpavan Brahmins who went to Poona from Shrivardhan in Kolaba district. Ratnagiri district in particular has produced noteworthy leaders of Maharashtra and of India.

Gokhale's father Krishnarao had sought service in Kagal a small feudatory state under Kolhapur State. He was employed there as a clerk and later became a sub-inspector of police; the salaries in the Princely states in those days were very meagre. Krishnarao's wife came from Kothik and belonged to the Oke family. They had six children, of whom two were boys. The elder was named Govind and the younger Gopal. Gopal Krishna Gokhale inherited his uprightness and habits of unselfish application from his family. He guarded this heritage scrupulously and left it richer for his life and career.

Very little is known about Gopal's school life in those early years, or his education at home. His mother was not educated, but she was full of wisdom and traditional knowledge. Stories from the epics, *Ramayana* and *Mahabharata,* were on her lips. So were the devotional songs of the saints and seers. Songs, fun of piety, love and ardour were sung early in the morning and late at night in the Gokhale household, diffusing purity and love. The impress left by these influences could be discerned in Gokhale in later years.

The house where Gopal was born, the school where he had his early education, the teachers who taught him, his comrades and friends in school, all are unknown. It is a matter of regret that no one has been able to throw light on this part of his life. All that we know about the boy at Kagal is that he completed his elementary education there. There is an anecdote repeated in the biographies, to which a reference should be made. Once his teacher set the boys a piece of homework in arithmetic. The answers of the other boys were wrong, only Gopal's was correct. The teacher asked him to move up to the top of the class. Instead of rejoicing over his promotion, he burst into tears. No one could understand the reason till he came out with the confession that the piece of homework had been solved not by him but by someone else.[3]

It must have been in 1874-75 that Gopal was sent to Kolhapur along with his brother for further studies. Kolhapur was the capital of a Princely state of the same name and was near Kagal. In those days only the larger towns like Kolhapur had schools teaching English. While the brothers were at Kolhapur, news came of the death of their father. Gopal was only 13 and his brother Govind 18. In a family of moderate means the demise of the earning member should normally have meant interruption of the boys studies. But

Gopal's uncle, Anantaji, took the widowed mother and her four daughters to Tamhanmala, though he himself was poor and had to maintain his own family. After a few months, Gopal's mother returned to Kagal with her daughters, determined to face the world on her own. In the altered circumstances it was settled that the elder brother should give up his education, and take up work, while the younger would stay at Kolhapur and complete his education. Through the good offices of relations, the elder was employed in a post at Kagal carrying Rs. 15 a month. It must have been very difficult for him to maintain the family and to provide for the education of his brother on such a low salary. Govind, who was only 18, agreed to send Rs. 8 out of the 15 rupees he was earning for the education and maintenance of Gopal at Kolhapur. It must have meant a hard life all round, full of self-denial. Gopal knew this well. It strengthened him in his resolve to make the best of this opportunity to succeed in life.

Out of Gopal's monthly allowance of Rs. 8, Rs. 4 went for food in an eating-house; the balance was spent on fees, books and clothes—an austere but character-forming life. He was conscious of the sufferings of his family and spent every pie with scrupulous care.

Once a class-mate asked him to go with him to a dramatic performance. Gopal agreed, went with him and witnessed the performance. After a day or two his friend asked him to pay for the ticket. Gopal was taken aback. If he had known that the show was going to cost him money, he would have courteously refused both the company and the pleasure. But self-respect asserted itself. He paid his friend the sum of two annas without argument or resentment. How was he to balance his budget? Could he gave up one more meal? Could he lay the axe on some other necessity? He decided to save on the kerosene needed for his lamp. He went out into the street and read his books under the street lamp.[4]

Gopal Krishna Gokhale passed the matriculation examination at the age of 15. But he had been prevailed upon to marry even before that. The celebration of a marriage cannot be understood unless it is home in mind that early marriages were the norm in those days. Society had not advanced far enough for anyone to disregard such a custom.

Young Gokhale got through his entrance examination at the first attempt. He won no scholarship and his name did not appear among the top-ranking students. The only notable fact is the comparatively early age at which he passed the examination. Although he had the desire, the ambition and the capacity for further studies, he thought it selfish to keep the family constantly in want for the sake of his higher education. He expressed a desire to start earning so as to cease to be a burden. But Govind would not hear of it, and Govind's wife too would not hear of young Gopal making such a sacrifice. She came forward with the offer to part with all her ornaments and jewellery for his education: Gokhale, was to join college. The country is indebted to Govind and his wife for giving Gokhale this opportunity to equip himself for the mission that awaited him in the country.[5]

Gokhale joined the Rajaram College at Kolhapur in January 1882. He was a shy student. Nothing much is known about his activities in college. He was alert but not brilliant.

He quickly gained a reputation in his college for exceptional retentiveness of memory. Srinivasa Sastri says, "Often he would lend a text-book to a mate and ask him to hold it while he went on reciting by heart. There used to be a bet, it would appear, that he should pay down an anna for every slip he made. Nobody made a fortune out of his mistakes."[6]

Although mastery of the English language was not one of his ambitions, any more than that of the young men of his time, he learnt to use it with sensitiveness and ability. His way was to commit good passages to memory. He could quote chapter and verse without a single mistake. It is said that he knew the whole of Scott's *Rokeby* by heart.[7] Some of his fellow students would tease him, calling him a crammer and a parrot, but Gokhale did not mind this.

In the Rajaram College he passed his previous examination, as it was then called, in 1882. For the second year's course he had to go to the Deccan College at Poona. But his stay in the Deccan College was short as the Rajararn College soon started the second year's course. He studied the first year of his B.A. course also in Kolhapur and then went to the Elphinstone College in Bombay for the final examination. He took mathematics as his optional subject and secured a second class.

That was in 1884. About 1880 very important events happened in Poona. The New English School was started by Vishnooshastri Chiplunkar. Next year, two weeklies, *Kesari* in Marathi and *Mahratta* in English, were started by Chiplunkar, Bal Gangadhar Tilak, Gopal Ganesh Agarkar and other young men. Certain letters were published in *Mahratta* on January 8, 1882, against one Barve, the Dewan of Kolhapur. *Kesari,* too, did not spare the Dewan. Tilak and Agarkar were sentenced to four months' imprisonment for defaming the Dewan as the letters ultimately turned out to be forged. The public sympathized with the editors and a fund for their defence was started. Students came out to collect the money. The New English School and the Deccan College raised about Rs. 400 for the fund. The Rajaram College of Kolhapur could not well lag behind. The students of the college staged a play in aid of the fund, Shakespeare's *Comedy of Errors.* Young Gokhale, who had remained aloof from all extra-curricular activities till then, agreed to play the part of the abbess in the play. This was his first appearance in public as a sympathizer in a political cause.[7]

In Bombay, where he went to study for his final examinations, Gokhale was attracted by Professor Hawthornwaite who was a renowned teacher in mathematics and a helpful guide. Dr Wordsworth, Professor of English, was another celebrity in the teaching world then. The two Englishmen influenced Gokhale greatly; they in turn were pleased with his accomplishments. He secured a scholarship of Rs. 20 a month.

Gokhale was admitted to the B.A. degree in 1884 at the age of 18, a rare achievement in those days. There were various choices before him. Should he register his name for the M.A. degree? Should he enter Government service? Should he join the law classes and became a lawyer? Some of his friends suggested that he should go to England to sit for the I.C.S. competitive examination. They promised to raise a loan for the purpose but Gokhale did not like the idea. It is possible that he thought that he was not equal to the task. Or possibly, he did not like the service. His final choice fell on engineering and he even enrolled his name in the Engineering College.

But when he saw how talented some of his classmates were, diffidence overcame him again and he stopped attending the classes. A plain M.A. degree holding was no attraction, he finally turned to law. To be a lawyer in those days was socially honourable and economically remunerative. One could even hope to enter the judiciary and became a High Court Judge, the highest position of eminence open to Indians then. A knowledge of law was desirable for other purposes as well. Gokhale might even have looked upon it as the right training ground for one who sought to serve his country.

Although he joined the law classes which started that year in the Deccan College at Poona, Gokhale could not forget his family which had gone through so much hardship for him. How long was he to keep them wafting for better days? Earning a living, therefore, became a necessity and a duty. Gokhale decided to accept the post of a teacher in the New English School, Poona, on a salary of Rs. 35 a month.

His life was inextricably mixed up with the events that were happening in Poona. When Gokhale chose the profession of teaching he had little idea of deliberately throwing himself into the vortex of events. But little by little he came to be a part of all that went on in Poona. Although he did not proclaim any flaming passion in fiery words, Gokhale in his own quiet way was as determined as his colleagues in the New English School on what the country needed.

For, the school in which he worked as a teacher was no ordinary school. It was not meant to turn out men who would be glorified clerks in the service of the foreign rulers. On the contrary, the founders of the school were persons determined to train a band of people rich in self-respect, learning and a sense of dedication. It was for such an institution that Gokhale laboured for no less than 15 years.

The architect of this school was Vishnooshastri Chiplunkar. He was a graduate who belonged to Poona. While in government service he was transferred to Ratnagiri from Poona as a teacher and was getting Rs. 100 a month, a decent salary in those days. He edited *Nibandhmala,* a periodical, in which thought-provoking articles appeared. It had caught the imagination of the educated class. In one of the essays, '*Amachya Deshachi Sthiti*' (the condition of our country), he expressed the opinion in unequivocal terms that education was the only way to regenerate the country. The essay was banned by the Government later as certain passages in it were considered highly objectionable.[8] Chiplunkar decided to resign from service and start a school at Poona. The school came into existence in the first month of 1880.

Tilak and Agarkar had also been thinking along the same lines even while studying in the Deccan College. India could only become free when her people were educated on modern lines: modern science, modern arts and modern ways of thinking alone would enable them to throw off the foreign yoke. Tilak remarked of himself and Agarkar that "their heads reeled with the depraved condition of the country, and that after prolonged thinking they had come to the conclusion that the uplift of the country depended upon education alone".[9] Tilak and Agarkar expressed a desire to join Chiplunkar's new venture. Some ridiculed them and called them visionaries. But the student world at large was waiting for the golden dawn. Chiplunkar said, "Rather than bend the knee to tyranny, I would snap asunder the chains once and for ever.[10]" The response to his pioneering attempt was splendid. Students vied with one another in enrolling their names. But the Government looked askance at this move. Chiplunkar showed prudence in not using high-sounding words while describing the object of the school in the opening address. He simply said that the object was to promote education by making it available even to persons of modest means. Chiplunkar, Tilak and G.M. Namjoshi took up the work. Agarkar did not join the school in the beginning as he wanted to complete his M.A. studies and asked for time to join the school.

Sacrifice and self-abnegation were necessary if the new venture was to succeed. The salary of these enthusiastic young men was only Rs. 30 to 35 a month. When more money was available they would start a chain of schools in Maharashtra but would not enhance their salaries. The ideal of sacrifice was thus both preached and practised. Poona was much taken up with the experiment. The Fergusson College was started in March 1885, the same year in which the Indian National Congress came into existence.

Gokhale was appointed as an assistant teacher on Rs. 35 a month in the New English School. That was too small a sum for his large family to live upon. He along with a teacher friend, started private classes for coaching students appearing for the Public Service examinations. Gokhale made about the same amount from these classes as his regular salary. An income of Rs. 70 or Rs. 75 a month was considered fairly handsome for a graduate of eighteen years of age. In his spare time he went for his legal studies. He passed the first examination. As there was no further provision for studying law at Poona he started going to Bombay to attend the Law College every week-end. But though he cherished the desire to be a lawyer, circumstances did not allow him to pursue law studies much longer.

The atmosphere in which his lot had been cast began to influence him profoundly. He came in contact with stalwarts like Tilak and Agarkar who were very ardent patriots. Subsequent events were to prove that Agarkar had greater influence on him than had Tilak. It was Agarkar, not Tilak, who prevailed upon him to join the staff as a life-member and be one amongst them. In the beginning, Gokhale seems to have hesitated somewhat, not because he did not want to join them but because his brother might object. Soon his brother's consent was obtained and Gokhale joined the ranks of these earnest persons in 1886. The foundation of his future was laid.

As a teacher, Gokhale did not make much of a mark. He taught English to the boys of the 4th and 5th standards. A successful scholar is not necessarily a successful teacher. But Gokhale was an indomitable optimist. He spared no pains to prepare for his classes. He would not refer to the text while teaching. Every sentence and every word was reproduced without notes. But his exposition of poetry went above the heads of the boys. They could not understand why their teacher was so enraptured by what appeared to them to be difficult words. The boys merely wanted the simple meaning of their English lessons but the teacher wanted them to reach the heart of the writers.

While in the Fergusson College, he had to teach Southey's *Life of Nelson.* It was not easy to teach it to Indian boys who had little knowledge of the sea, of ships and docks, and of naval life. It was characteristic of his thoroughness that Gokhale went to Bombay and visited the docks to learn the nautical terms and phrases.[11]

In the first year of his career in the tutorial line, Gokhale seems to have decided to achieve as much command as possible over the intricacies of the English language. He further developed his habit of committing to memory the writings of the best authors. Among the literary masterpieces memorized by him were Milton's *Paradise Lost* and the speeches of Burke, Gladstone, John Bright and several other British orators and parliamentarians. He would seek a lonely place and declaim them by himself, rarely committing a mistake. Editorials by English editors did not escape his attention.

Gokhale's method of training himself helped him in other ways also. While he studied the great spirits of literature and liberalism mainly to improve his scholarship and powers of analysis, they were to stand him in good stead in his later career as legislator and statesman.

In the New English School, Gokhale taught not only English but mathematics and other subjects as occasion arose. While teaching arithmetic in the school in 1886-87 the idea occurred to him that he should compile a text book on the subject. In those days, and even later, professors in the Fergusson College were asked to teach in the New English School as well. Gokhale came to be acquainted with N.J. Bapat, who was a very good teacher in the subject. Together, the two compiled a book which Gokhale showed to Tilak, who was then Professor of Mathematics. Tilak liked it and encouraged him to find a publisher. It was prescribed as a textbook in the New English School even before it was printed. The book was useful and popular and was prescribed by many schools in India. It ran through a number of editions and had a large sale. Its publication was a boon to Gokhale. It is said that he secured about Rs. 1,500 a year from the publishers as royalty. It was first published in English but was later translated into other languages as well.[12]

Though Gokhale was now fairly well settled in life, all was not well in the Society of which he had become a life-member. Trouble was brewing ever since Gokhale joined the Society. It is necessary to understand the cross-currents and under-currents that agitated this premier Society and had their repercussions on public life in Maharashtra, and indirectly on India. Vishnooshastri Chiplunkar, the founder of the School, died a premature death, on March 17, 1882, at the age of 32. In July 1882, Agarkar and Tilak were sentenced to four months' imprisonment in the defamation case that the Dewan of Kolhapur brought against them. On October 24, 1884, the Deccan Education Society was formed. On January 22, 1885, the Fergusson College was inaugurated. On October 14, 1890, Tilak resigned his life-membership of the Society. These are important dates in the history of the Deccan Education Society. The details of the conflict need not detain us. But we should have a broad picture of the happenings. For the lives of Tilak and Gokhale had roots in the Society: they both became leaders of all-India fame; they moulded the destinies of the country. But they had fundamental differences as well which were reflected in a painful manner, early in their relationship.

Tilak and Agarkar were considered to be inseparables in their student days and in the Society of which they were founders. They were to the fore in the fight for the liberation of the country. Agarkar, however, laid great emphasis on social reform as on political changes. Tilak, though was not opposed to changes in social matters, held that political freedom should precede social reforms. These two, along with another friend, had started *Kesari* and *Mahratta.* Tilak was in-charge of *Kesari,* and Agarkar of *Mahratta.* On many occasions divergent views came to be expressed in the two weeklies. The differences grew and the editors were affected by them.

Another reason for the split was that both of them were insistent on following the principles of sacrifice and suffering laid down by the Jesuits. But differences arose in the application of the principles. A proper balance had to be struck between the ideal and the practical. Tilak in his memorable letter of resignation in 1890 fully dealt with the subject. He said that in spite of several suggestions by him for compromise, no way out could be found. The point at issue related to salaries and incomes. Should a life-member earn outside the Society also and thus fritter away his energies? Will not such outside work come in the way of his efficient teaching? These and similar questions had made work in the Society difficult.[13]

Tilak said that he did not expect the members of the staff to be ascetics. They were given a salary of Rs. 75 a month, a bonus of Rs. 400 a year, as also a life insurance policy for Rs. 3,000. A life-member was to get his salary till the end of his life. These arrangements sound reasonable; yet equal pay for all does not seem to have found favour with some of the members. Tilak's contention was that they were all engaged in the same mission. There should be no privations, neither should there be heart-burning over unequal pay.

Misunderstandings led to serious differences. Tilak said in his letter of resignation: "The only way to get out of these difficulties is to stop outside work altogether, or rule that the profits thereof shall go to the common fund as is the case in the missionary societies."[14] In the same letter Tilak said of the new members that they appeared to believe that life-membership was a good start for a beginner in Poona and that if one had energy and ambition, one could use it "as a stepping-stone for personal distinction and gain."[15] Tilak came to be called a stoic and his disinterestedness was looked upon as a cloak for self-assertion and self-glorification. The only course left for Tilak was to resign, which he did.

The proximate cause of the resignation can be seen from the following incident. Matters came to a head when Gokhale intended to accept the secretaryship of the Sarvajanik Sabha. On July 25, Tilak addressed a letter to the secretary of the managing body of the Deccan Education Society, proposing a meeting. He said, "I know that Mr. Gokhale has been allowed to do private work to supplement his income to a certain extent. But I think a distinction should be made between occasional private work and accepting permanent service and responsibility elsewhere. I think it is inconsistent with our object and contrary to the understanding which brought us together."[16]

The meeting was called and a resolution was moved by Tilak, disapproving the impending acceptance of the secretaryship of the Sarvajanik Sabha by Gokhale. Five voted for it and four against. Agarkar and Gokbale were in the minority. At the same meeting, another resolution approving Gokhale's acceptance was passed with 5 votes for and 4 against. Patankar, who was with Tilak at first, had changed sides. Thus a piquant situation arose: Gokhale was both free and not free to accept the post. Tilak reopened the question and another meeting was called on October 14. At that meeting Prof. Kelkar moved a resolution which was in effect against the acceptance of the secretaryship by Gokhale. Kelkar's resolution was passed with 6 votes for and 3 against. After this resolution was passed, Agarkar moved that it applied to all including himself. Votes were taken as to which members the resolution was applicable but the voting was puzzling. Tilak, Agarkar, Namjoshi and Apte were singled out as persons to whom the resolution was applicable. The original resolution thus affected Tilak. He immediately resigned, promising a detailed statement later. The Society was divided against itself. Gokhale had already taken up the post of the secretary and it was left to his good sense to continue or not to continue as a member of the Society."[17]

After Tilak's resignation, another letter by Gokhale followed on the same day and at the same meeting. Gokhale said that if his withdrawal from the Society could induce Tilak to remain, "I offer my resignation as a life-member." Gokhale was told that Tilak's resignation was not connected with Gokhale's connection or severance from the Deccan Education Society. Gokhale thereupon withdrew his resignation. Patankar also tendered his resignation along with Tilak and this was accepted. Thus ended the most painful chapter in the history of the Society which had set out to teach the lessons of sacrifice and suffering to the people at large.

The Deccan Education Society continued to flourish and promote education. Many educational institutions owe their inception to this organization whose members were inspired by a sense of sacrifice. And leaders of the Society tried to avoid clashes with the Government by adopting a policy of moderation, sobriety and conciliation.

Gokhale and Tilak were both great men meant for a wider arena than the Society. Years later, Gokhale started the 'Servants of India Society' the members of which were precluded from taking up activities outside that Society. Anything they earned over and above their prescribed incomes was credited to the Society. Gokhale carried out the Jesuit principle of sacrifice for the common good scrupulously in the institution which he founded, though he could not do so in the Deccan Education Society.

Tilak was not the founder of any more societies or institutions where such principles were to be observed strictly. But the *Kesari* and the *Mahratta* attracted men of sacrifice who were great in their own way. Tilak was the proprietor of these concerns which were rarely out of monetary difficulties. He could not give the members of the staff the salaries they deserved. Nor was the principle of anything earned outside being credited to the principal body ever professed. Outside activities, on the other band, enhanced the prestige of the weeklies and added to their strength.

To the members of the Deccan Education Society, India was a country to be liberated from foreign domination by making the people self-reliant and discerning through education. Tilak, Agarkar and their colleagues were practical men. They knew that for the country's regeneration the spirit of sacrifice was needed and not the letter of it. After all, what was important? Was it the spirit of sacrifice for educating the people, or was sacrifice an end in itself? Gokhale had not thought deeply about these things and he was in search of a guide. Agarkar appealed to him more than Tilak. Gokhale was only sorry that he was the cause of widening the rift and bringing matters to a head. He wanted to leave the Society but his going away would not have brought about harmony in the organization. In all this, he showed that he was simple, frank and unassuming.

REFERENCES

1. Deogirikar, T.R., *Gopal Krishna Gokhale* (New Delhi: Publications Division, Ministry of Information and Broadcasting, Government of India), 1950.
2. Chirol Valentine, *The Indian Unrest* (London: Macmillan), 1910.
3. Parvate, T.V., *Gopal Krishna Gokhale* (Ahmedabad: Navajivan Publishing House), 1958, pp. 22-23.
4. *Ibid.*, p. 11.
5. *Ibid.*
6. Sastri, V.S.S., *Life of Gopal Krishna Gokhale* (Bangalore: Bangalore Printing Co.), 1937, p. 5.
7. Nanda, B.R., *Gokhale* (Delhi: Oxford University Press), 1977, p. 6.

8. Deogirikar, T.R., *Gopal Krishna, op. cit.*, pp. 10-11.
9. Nanda, B.R., *Gokhale, op. cit.*, p. 29.
10. Deogirikar, T.R., *Gopal Krishna, op. cit.*, p. 14.
11. *Ibid.*
12. Parvate, T.V., *Gopal Krishna Gokhale op. cit.*, p. 19.
13. Deogirikar, T.R., *Gopal Krishna, op. cit.*, p. 17.
14. Nanda, B.R., *Three Statesmen: Gokhale, Gandhi and Nehru* (Delhi: Oxford University Press), 2004, pp. 26-38.
15. *Ibid.*
16. *Ibid.*
17. Deogirikar, T.R., *Gopal Krishna, op. cit.*, p. 19.

2

IDEOLOGY AND PERCEPTION

Gokhale chose for his special extra-curricular interest the field of political activity and reform, He became Secretary of the Bombay Provincial Conference in 1888. Such conferences as supporting organizations of the Indian National Congress were then being set up in the several provinces. As Secretary of one of the most active and influential among these bodies, Gokhale commenced the career of an Indian Congressman in which he was to find the fulfilment of his life's mission. In the same year, 1888, Gokhale accepted responsibility as Editor of the English side of an Anglo-Marathi weekly journal, called *Sudharak* (Reformer) of which Gopal Ganesh Agarkar, the famous social reformer of Maharashtra and a founder of the Deccan Education Society, was the Chief Editor.

The Sudharak was essentially a non-sectarian journal devoted to bringing about comprehensive reformation among the people of India. Freedom and equality among men were held to be essential pre-conditions of individual and national progress. It was in this concept that education, in its wider sense, was sought to be promoted as the chief instrument of national regeneration. In fact, such journals were in the thinking of the founders of the Deccan Education Society, a necessary supplement to their scholastic activities. Neither Agarkar nor Gokhale recognized any limits to the ambitions and aspirations of their nations. They felt convinced, however, that unless the institutional framework of Indian society was recognized so as to free the individual from restrictive social practices, the fullest realization of the potentialities of Indian progress in the modern age would not be possible. Like education, freedom also must be carried to all members of the society, irrespective of class, creed or sex, if humanity is to grow to the highest limits of its capacity.

Western Influence

Both as student and teacher, Gokhale was influenced by the writings of eminent British philosophers and statesmen. Of these John Stuart Mill and Edmund Burke appeared to have been most favoured. Many of Gokhale's ideas which lay at the root of his appreciations and suggestions concerning current problems were derived from such classics as Mill's Essays on Liberty and Representative Government and Burke's Reflections on the French Revolution. The moral revolt against the degrading effect of foreign autocracy, which Gokhale personified, was fully sanctioned, if not initially suggested, by Mill's ideas on the dignity of man and progress of society.[1] The clear understanding of the process of constitutional change, and in particular appreciation of the healthy and lasting results of gradual reform were contributions of Burke. The trait of moderation commonly attributed to Gokhale is referable only to what he considered to be an acceptable next step towards his goal of limitless progress for the individual and the society. The words which Gokhale used in controversial discussions were generally soft and in this respect he was inclined to share the well-known British trait of habitual understatement.

Public Platform

The virtue of gradualism so favoured by Gokhale is fully illustrated by his own career of increasingly important positions held by him and by the expanding sphere of his service to the nation. In the very first year of his career as a recognized public worker, he made three important speeches. Of these one was concerned with what may have normally passed as no more than an anti-corruption case against a senior official of the Government of Bombay, to wit Mr. Crawford, Commissioner, Central Division.[2] But when legal proceedings instituted against this official by the Government were sought to be stalled and sabotaged on racial grounds it became necessary for public-spirited citizens to come out with strong support for official action to uphold purity in public administration, irrespective of considerations of race. Gokhale harped on this theme of racial equality in India and elsewhere in the British Empire, throughout his life.

In the same year, in 1889, Gokhale made his debut on the Congress platform. It is not without some stirrings of political and personal interest that one notices the fact that Gokhale's very first contribution to a public debate from the Congress platform, on a subject of constitutional reform in India, was in the shape of seconding an amendment proposed by Tilak.[3] The official resolution was in support of a scheme of Council Reform in which it was suggested that Provincial representatives on the Supreme Legislative Council should be elected directly by Municipal and Local Boards. Tilak's amendment amounted to a narrowing of the electorate to the elected members of the Provincial Councils. There was much to be said in favour of this more indirect method of election, and between them, Gokhale and Tilak said it. But this amendment was lost. Gokhale had many a future occasion of success within the Congress. But his subsequent avowal that his generation must be content to serve their countrymen more by their failures than by their successes appears to have an origin going as far back as his very first participation in public debate. His second participation in a Congress discussion, that on a resolution concerning the Indian Public Services was more favourably received. Gokhale continued to take a lively and a serious interest in the Indianization of Public Services, which he considered to be essential politically, economically and culturally, Even at the time of his death he was a member of a Royal Commission on Public Services in India.

Institutional Responsibilities

Gradually, however, Gokhale came to occupy more responsible positions and his participation in public debates, both within and outside the Congress came to be received with greater respect. In the year 1890, he became Secretary of the Poona Sarvajanik Sabha which was then among the foremost of India's public associations for political work. In addition to his duties as Secretary, Gokhale assumed responsibilities as Editor of the quarterly Journal of Sabha. Among the contributors of this Journal were persons like Ranade and G.V. Joshi, the Hatter being the first Indian publicist to make significant use of official statistics in support of popular representation of views. Gokhale was to receive in later years almost as much collaboration from Joshi as he received guidance from Ranade. During the next year, Gokhale had to take up more organizing responsibility within the Deccan Education Society of which body he then became the Secretary. He added further to his educational responsibility in 1895, when he became Fellow of the University of Bombay. But that year was to be more significant in Gokhale's political career as a Congressman. He was Secretary of the Reception Committee of the Poona session of the Congress. It may be recalled that the very first session of the Congress was to have been held in Poona, but due to the prevalence of plague in that city that plan had to be dropped.

Justice to India

At an earlier session of the Congress (1893), speaking of the Indian Councils Act, 1892, Gokhale made some important observations, which he often referred to in later years. Those related mostly to subjects like expansion of Councils, especially of the non-official and elected elements in them, and conferring upon them more positive functions in respect of the budget and of moving resolutions on measures of public importance. A more important speech of that year was, however, the one on Home Military Charges delivered by Gokhale at a public meeting in Bombay presided over by Pherozeshah Mehta. In moving the adoption of a memorial on the subject to be submitted to the British House of Commons, Gokhale brought his remarks to a close with the following observations:

"Gentlemen, England is strong, but let her not abuse her strength by extorting from poor India more than she has a right to receive. England professes to be anxious to do justice to India. We have had nearly a century these professions and it is now time we had a little of the practice of the thing."[4]

The Deccan Sabha

The years that followed the Poona session of the Congress were critical years in Gokhale's advance to political leadership. In 1896 along with his Guru, Ranade, and other prominent members of the Sarvajanik Sabha, Gokhale resigned membership of that body. Apart from a clash of personalities, which is occasionally unavoidable in popularly organized bodies, the principal ground for this serious split was one which was destined in later years to cause a continuing division among public men in Maharashtra, and in India as a whole. The Ranade group, to which Gokhale devoted his allegiance, believed that at the current stage of the country's growth a policy of popular education, more equalitarian and more progressive reconstruction of social institutions, and a steady building up of national political organization should have priority over campaigning for active opposition to the British Government. The other view that the first priority of public activities in a dependent country is to attain national independence at any cost was gradually attracting support among members of the Sarvajanik Sabha. To give both schools of thought full opportunity to work in support of their respective programmes, the adherents of the Ranade, or the Liberal and Moderate school, left the old Sabha, and constituted a new body, called the Deccan Sabha, of which Gokhale became the first Secretary.

The Manifesto issued by the new body contains an enunciation of the principle characteristics of programmes of action which its members sought to promote. The most significant part of this Manifesto, which is said to have been drawn up by Ranade himself, runs as follows:

"The spirit of Liberalism implies a freedom from race and creed prejudices and a steady devotion to all that seeks to do justice between man and man, giving to the rulers the loyalty that is due to the law they are bound to administer, but securing at the same time to the ruled the equality which is their right under the law. Moderation imposes the condition of never vainly aspiring after the impossible or after too remote ideals, but striving each day to take the next step in the order of natural growth by doing the work that lies nearest to our hands in a spirit of compromise and fairness. After all, political activities are chiefly of value not for the particular results achieved, but for the process of political education which is secured by exciting interest in public matters and promoting the self-respect and self-reliance of citizenship. This is no doubt a slow process but all growth of new habits must be slow to be real."[5]

First Meeting with Gandhi

The ideals, values and methods of political life inscribed in this declaration were to play a determining role in shaping Gokhale's own views on public questions, and in influencing his relations with the representatives of the British Government on the one hand and with the leaders of several political groups within the country on the other. It is noteworthy that it was exactly at this stage in the career of Gokhale, and in fact at the very moment when the principles of the party Liberalism and Moderation were taking shape, that Gandhi had his first meeting with Gokhale. What Gandhi was then primarily interested in was to seek the support of Indian public men for the struggle which the Natal Indian Congress was waging against the Colonial Government to secure their rights as settlers. The "freedom from race and creed prejudices," and "the equality under the law" incorporated in the Manifesto were not mere empty words for Gokhale. He was prepared to back them with active support, whether it was in India or Natal. It was this first meeting between the two that laid the foundation of an abiding intimacy which was richly valued on either side.

Gokhale's first visit to England was undertaken in 1897 for the purpose of tendering evidence before the Welby Commission on behalf of the Deccan Sabha. The high merit of both the written and the oral testimony presented by him had been appreciated on all sides. Gokhale soon came to be recognized as one among the few well-informed and responsible exponents of the Indian view on public finance and administration in India. This first visit of Gokhale to England was, also, destined to be of great historical interest for the future of the political relationship between India and Great Britain. Like many a young graduate, Gokhale was well steeped in the words of great liberal philosophers of England. Both for his own writings, and for his interpretation of the thoughts of other liberal philosophers and statesmen, Morley had a special attraction for educated Indians. At least in part he was their inspirer of a love for political liberty and their source of reassurance that under England's overall protection they would attain to that happy stage.

The Liberal Party of Great Britain, then in opposition, lent special prestige to them as friends and collaborators of those Indians who were striving to ensure the early realization of British pledges to India. When he was in England, Gokhale called on Morley and attempted, among other things, to interest him and, through him, the Liberal Party in the activities of Indian politicians. From what Sir William Wedderburn, one time President of the Congress and always its most prominent exponent in U.K., said later on this initial contact between Gokhale and Morley, seems to have been partially responsible for Morley's acceptance of the India portfolio when it was offered to him several years later. It is more than probable that this circumstance influenced Gokhale in his attitude of obvious prepossession for and confidence in Morley and the British Liberal Party.

Gandhi's briefing on the position of Indians in South Africa had not been neglected by Gokhale was borne out by the publication, in the same year, of an article of his in the India Quarterly published in London. The main theme of the article was insistence on securing equality of treatment among citizens of all the races which constituted the British Empire, In normal circumstances with memories of the Welby Commission, meeting with Morley and other leaders in U.K., and publicity to the plight of Indians in South Africa, Gokhale should have returned in contentment, if not in triumph, to India. Instead, as luck would have it, he had to face the severest trial of his career in the very hour of his setting foot on the Indian soil.

Apology Incident

He had felt it to be his duty as a public man to stand up for his countrymen, when he was in England. The need for bold action had arisen in two somewhat divergent ways. On the one hand, several friends from Poona, whose sense of responsibility he had then no cause to doubt, had written to him complaining in specific terms of the high-handedness and misbehaviour of some among those who were in charge of anti-plague measures in Poona. On the other hand, Indian correspondents of British papers and several writers in the British Press were severely criticizing leaders in India, especially those in Poona, for their lack of a sense of loyalty and responsibility. As a public man Gokhale felt it to be his duty to vindicate his own and his colleagues' reputation for loyalty and responsibility, and also to place before the British public the kind of happenings in Poona which had created an unusual stir in the Indian mind. In doing this he was acting as an honest public leader. His reference to the atrocities committed by some British soldiers in the course of the execution of their duties had created a wave of resentment in England. It was this that had also roused the wrath of the whole Anglo-Indian community. When on his return Gokhale found that his private correspondents on whose information he had relied, were unable or unwilling to substantiate their complaints, the only course open to him, as a gentleman, and as a respectable public man was to tender an apology. An apology, which is worth anything either to the giver or to the receiver, has to be a full and unqualified one, and it has to be addressed to those who are the real sufferers of the wrong that is sought to be corrected by the apology. Gokhale rose magnificently to the occasion and thereby enhanced his own worth as a man and as a respectable leader of his countrymen. That in doing so he earned the odium of a large number of his less informed and less conscientious countrymen, was the penance he had to go through to attain the sublimity of his "Righteousness" which struck a responsive chord in Gandhi and Sarojini Naidu.[6]

After the apology, characteristically enough, it was the plague in Poona which attracted his first attention. He took active and energetic part in organizing relief for the victims and their relations. As he gradually recovered his mental calm and took up the threads of numerous public activities, he found much in his environment to encourage him to further his efforts on national service. In 1899 he was elected a member of the Bombay Legislative Council. Gokhale always had more than his average share of a sense of public responsibility. When later on, in 1903, he was elected Joint General

Secretary of the Congress, he toured the country delivering public speeches on current political problems. After his retirement from the Fergusson College in 1902, which also was the year in which he was elected President of the Poona Municipality, Gokhale became almost a whole-time worker for the Congress. Whatever he did in India or abroad was done largely on behalf of the Congress.

Bombay Legislative Council

He spent only a short span of two years as a member of the Bombay Legislative Council. During his term of membership when the Mofussil Municipalities Bill came up for discussion, Gokhale made an important speech in the course of which he had to declare his views both on the nature of Municipal Government and on the provision of communal electorates contained in the Bill. He observed:

"We value local self-government not only for the fact that local work thereby is better done, but also for the fact that it teaches men of different castes and creeds, who have long been kept more or less apart, to work together for a common purpose. There are in all conscience causes differences enough among the different sections of this land, and I submit that the legislature should not, in the best interest of the country, without the very strongest reasons, give any statutory recognition to these differences. There is nothing in the nature of local self-government which implies any conflict between the interests of one section and another. If the Council will turn to the list of "obligatory duties" and "optional duties" it will be seen that except perhaps on the question of slaughter houses there is no chance of conflict of interest arising between the different communities. And on that particular question, if the Hindu Councillors anywhere neglected to construct slaughter houses for the benefit of Mohamedans and other inhabitants, Government have it in their power, under the provisions of the "Control Chapter", to require recalcitrant municipalities to perform that duty. Then, if different sections are to be represented, why talk of the Hindu Community as a whole by itself? There are, so many castes and sections of the community, and some of them can stand apart from one another, that it will be necessary to recognize their differences. Under such circumstences, where is the Government going to stop?[7]

What Gokhale thought as an unsound and almost absurd formula was ultimately retained in the Act. When, later on, the electoral principle was accepted for legislative councils, even what Gokhale thought were absurd limits of carrying communal representation to castes among the Hindus were also reached. It is only fair to add that in this speech Gokhale ended his remarks by stating: "I have no objection to Government providing for sectional representation by means of election, provided they guarantee to the general rate-payers a minimum of half the seats." But the first pronouncement of Gokhale on the subject of communal representation brings out his general position, in clear terms. Another part of his speech on the same Bill brings out his views on the important subject of separation of powers. While he upholds the principle of an executive separate from the deliberative body of the Municipal Council for large cities like Bombay, he favours the conferment of executive functions on popular bodies in the smaller mofussil towns.[8]

Imperial Legislative Council

When in December 1903, an Amending Bill was moved in the Imperial Legislative Council to extend the scope of the Official Secrets Act of 1889 to cover even civil information, in addition to information bearing on military matters to which the original Act referred, Gokhale had an important speech to make both on the first and second readings. Gokhale was a member of the Select Committee set up to consider the Amending Bill. Along with two other non-official members, Bose and Nawab Saiyyad Mahammud, Gokhale had appended a minute of dissent to the Select Committees Report. Speaking about the minute Gokhale said:

"We have expressed that dissent in the mildest terms which we could possibly find to convey our meaning. We did this both to mark our sense of the conciliatory manner in which the Hon'ble Member-in-charge of the Bill received many of our suggestions and in the hope that by thus removing from our dissent all trace of the angry criticisms to which the Bill has been subjected, we might make it easier for Government to proceed further in the direction of meeting the objections urged by the public."[9]

In spite of this gentle technique, which was always characteristic of Gokhale, way, no further concessions were made by the Government. Intervening later in the course of discussion Gokhale was constrained to observe:

"Nowhere throughout the British Empire is the Government so powerful relatively to the governed as in India. Nowhere, on the other hand, is the Press so weak in influence as it is with us. The vigilance of the Press is the only check that operates from outside, feebly, it is true but continuously, upon the conduct of the Government, which is subject to no popular control. It is here, therefore, if anywhere, that the Legislature should show special consideration to the Press, and yet here alone it is proposed to arm Government with greater power to control the freedom of the Press than in any other part of the Empire."[10]

Work of the Congress

In the Congress session held at Madras, in December 1903, Gokhale, who was to be present, was elected Joint General Secretary. His elevation to this official position in the non-official Parliament of the Indian people made him forget even more completely than before all thought of everything except service of the country through the Congress. Speaking at Madras in July 1904, he reviewed the history of the Congress during its existence of about twenty years, and asserted that considering the difficulties in their way, the position of strength occupied by the British bureaucracy in India and the many weaknesses among its people, they had indeed not done badly. Alluding to the recent rise of Japan, especially its industrial progress, he insisted on the inner unity between political and industrial advance and urged his countrymen to emulate the Japanese in their patriotism and discipline. He felt convinced that if the Congress persisted with greater vigour and tenacity in the task of political education, and organization of the people, they would soon attain the freedom and welfare of the country as a self-governing part of the British Empire. Speaking about the people who indulge in counsels of despair, he said:

"Those who say that nothing is to be gained by political agitation they really do a great disservice to the country; they do nothing themselves and they only paralyse the efforts of others. It is said that history furnishes no example of a subject people rising by such methods as ours. I have myself paid some attention to history; and if I have been convinced of one thing more than another, it is this: that you can never have a perfect, parallel in history. It is impossible for circumstances to repeat themselves, though you have the common saying that history repeats itself. It may be that the history of the world does not furnish an instance where a subject race has risen by agitation. If so, we shall supply that example for the first time. The history of the world has not yet come to an end; there are more chapters to be added."[11]

During the remainder of his life of a decade or so, Gokhale himself added a few brilliant chapters, though the most significant of all was left to be added by his "younger brother"[12] and his stalwart supporters. Even in this speech, Gokhale showed a keen awareness of the need to have greater discipline and devotion in the political life of the country.

"The day has gone by," he said, "when politics could afford to be amateurish in this land. It has been amateurish in the past; but the struggle is growing keener and keener and it is necessary that men should take up the duties and responsibilities of public life in life in the same manner as they choose their profession and devote their energies to it."[13]

It is obvious that the need to have in each State at least a small band of devoted and dedicated public workers which was engaging Gokhale's thought for some years past, was now assuming a more definite shape. Within less than a year of this speech in Madras, on June 12, 1905 at Poona, Gokhale administered the vows of membership to three of his colleagues along with whom he founded the Servants of India Society.

Several years later Jawaharlal Nehru observed in his *Discovery of India:* "Gopal Krishna Gokhale once wrote in his gently ironical way of the inscrutable wisdom of Providence which had ordained the British connection for India. Whether it was due to this inscrutable wisdom or some process of historic destiny or just chance, the coming of the British to India brought two very different races together."[14] Every student of history, most of all every great man, is entitled to read and interpret history in his own way. But quite, obviously when Jawaharlal Nehru traced a gentle irony in Gokhale's avowal of the inscrutable wisdom of Providence, the full facts about Gokhale's philosophical and moral position could not have been placed before him. Gokhale was gentle, indeed sometimes very gentle. But he was never ironical, least of all about Providence. His faith in a Providence governing the destinies of men and nations was not a mere short-cut or euphemism for chance. He believed, as did Ranade, in a benevolent influence guiding the life of the world. Wisdom and benevolence were attributes of Providence which both were content to accept, though certain happenings in themselves may not be so easily explicable to the limited knowledge of even the most knowing and far-sighted among men. Gokhale, in fact, following Ranade, rationalized to his satisfaction, the implied benevolence of "the coming of the British to India." Against the background of India's political and cultural history both of them felt that contact with the modern world of science and organization, as also with the political values of freedom and a national state was indispensable for a national movement of regeneration in India. There may be legitimate criticisms of this view, but it was not ironically conceived. In much of the programme of practical action indicated for members, the implications of this view were clearly spelt out. Indeed, many of these items were adopted, in mass or in detail, by a number of other organizations as well. Later on when Gandhi outlined his constructive programme some of the tasks prescribed by Gokhale for his colleagues were incorporated in it.[15]

Mission in England

Soon after the establishment of the Servants of India Society, Gokhale undertook a visit to England on behalf of the Congress. His mission, on this second journey to U.K., was to explain to the British people the state of public feeling in India regarding the repressive acts of the regime of Lord Curzon, and in particular about the crowning piece of his arrogant disregard of Indian public opinion, the partition of Bengal. As it happened, that was also the time when a fresh General Election was to be held in U.K. and the Liberal Party which in opposition had shown sympathetic interest in India's claims to progressive self-government was expected to come into power. Curzon personified the stony and cold attitude which the entire bureaucratic government of India had adopted towards the demands of the Congress. Discontent was daily becoming, more and more widespread and a crisis in Indo-British relations and in the internal political movement in India was fast developing. Leaders of the Congress, at least some among them, felt that if India's case was at this juncture placed before the British public and the new British Government, the crisis may be forestalled. This was a delicate and by no means a very hopeful mission. The choice of Gokhale to carry it out, and his acceptance of the responsibility are indicative on the one hand of the great confidence placed in his patriotism and statesmanship by his colleagues and, on the other hand, of a fully restored vigour and balance of mind of Gokhale himself.

The most challenging assignment of the tour was a speech in Manchester on Indian Discontent. It is true that Manchester was a stronghold of Liberalism and as such had a receptive atmosphere, so far as the general political theme is concerned. But the agitation for boycott of British goods started in Bengal had disturbed the mood of all connected with the British textile trade and even some of the friends of India in Great Britain attempted to dissuade Gokhale from undertaking the Manchester assignment. Gokhale, however, was keen on explaining to the politically active section of the population of Manchester the real significance of the boycott of British cloth. He made it clear to his audience that the boycott did not signify on the part of the people of India any animosity either against Great Britain, in general, or against Manchester, in particular. He recounted with his characteristic lucidity the background and the ugly features of the whole scheme of partition. He told them how all avenues of normal constitutional agitation in India and in Britain had been exhausted. An effective appeal to the British public could thus be made against the perverse policy of the bureaucracy in India and the British Government of the day in no other peaceful way than the boycott which all classes of people in Bengal had spontaneously adopted. This speech, far from being resented by the listeners, marked the beginning of a definite change in the attitude of the Liberal Party towards the Partition issue.[16]

The really important group of speeches was, however, addressed to more sophisticated audiences in London. On some of these occasions also, Gokhale had to speak before informed and interested but by no means very sympathetic gatherings. His address to the East India Association on Self-Government for India must have been jarring to the ears of at least some die-hards in the audience. In fact Gokhale felt called upon at the end of his speech to thank the Association all the more heartily because of this recognized dis-agreement. But it was exactly on such occasions that the respectful, objective and firm style of Gokhale ensured for him a substantially courteous reception. Moreover, even if no immediate agreement was obtained, the seeds of doubt and faint stirrings of second thoughts were planted in the minds of several members of the opposition. This is exactly why the British bureaucrats in India disliked these visits of Gokhale which ensured for him notable reception both in the British Press and among the leaders of Parliamentary opinion. Gokhale invariably appealed to the conscience, the feeling of honour and the high constitutional principles of the British people. He successfully turned the ire of the British people to their bureaucratic representatives in India by stating:

"There is no doubt that the old faith of the people in the character and ideals of British rule has been more than shaken and its place is being steadily taken by a conviction that however great England may be, she is not great enough to forego voluntarily the gains of power from considerations of mere justice or national honour. I do not say that such a view is quite just to the average man or woman of this country ... but the people of India can judge of the intentions of Englishmen only from their experience of those who go out to India to excise authority over them."[17]

He reminded his audience that "After all, India's willing acceptance of the British connection can only be based on reason or enlightened self-interest." He went on to assert that, "They want their country to be a prosperous, self-governing integral part of the Empire, like the Colonies, and not a mere poverty-stricken, bureaucratically held possession of that Empire." The full significance of this speech can be realized if we note that it was made in England to an audience of retired Anglo-Indian bureaucrats and their mostly conservative backers well before the Calcutta Congress at which *Swaraj*, that is the status of a self-governing colony of the Empire, was declared to be goal of the Congress. It was after this claim to freedom and prosperity on behalf of his countrymen that Gokhale uttered his grave warning to the British people:

"And here I repeat that unless the old faith of the educated classes character and ideals of British rule is brought back, England will find on her hands before long another Ireland, only many times bigger in India."[18]

By comparison his other speeches on the need for political reform were addressed to more friendly audiences in London. Speaking at the Liberal Club on England's Duty towards India, the natural ideological alliance between Indian reformers and British, he urged on them as the new Party in power to proceed firmly with the task of reconciliation and reconstruction in India, which was neglected after Lord Ripon had laid the foundations of local self-government. The absurd anomaly of wooing Japanese support against Russia, while alienating the Indian people, needed an early correction. So did the policy of racial discrimination against coloured inhabitants and settlers in Crown colonies like Transvaal, which in this respect were often worse than the self-governing colonies like Natal.[19]

Speaking to the New Reform Club in November 1905, Gokhale recounted the full story of Lord Curzon's complete undoing of all the assurances of the British Sovereign and of the aspirations of the Indian people. Racial discrimination in the due process of law and in the services, suppression of the liberties of citizens, officialization of university managements and reduction of the powers of local self-governing bodies were only a few of the several measures of his regime which had created an explosive situation in

India. The moral which Gokhale derived from this story, for himself and for the well-meaning among the British people, was that so long as the system of foreign bureaucratic rule has not been replaced by Indian self-government, the declared goals of British policy in India will not be realized. Having made the declarations of racial equality and given the assurances of equal protection of laws, having started modern institutions of education and government, England ought not to flinch from taking the crucial steps forward, long ago anticipated by Macaulay and Ripon. The system of government where supreme power is vested in persons who are only temporary residents of the country was unnatural.

> The only solution that is possible—a solution demanded alike by our interests and by your interests, as also by your national honour—is the steady introduction of self-government in India.[20]

The echoes of several sentiments expressed by Gokhale in the course of his public speeches in England on this occasion (1905) are clearly traceable in later correspondence and pronouncements of Morley and Minto. In fact it is doubtful whether in the absence of the favourable background and opinion created by Gokhale, the reforms of 1909 could have been incorporated into the parliamentary programme of the new Liberal Government in Great Britain. Not only in the acceptance of the urgent need for political reform but in regard to at least some of the broad outlines of the constitutional scheme Gokhale's influence was unmistakable.

President of the Congress

The most important political speech which Gokhale made in this eventful year (1905) was his address as President of the Congress session held at Banaras. Not only the fact that he attained the honour of this high position at a comparatively young age, but the unerring justice of his observations and the broad vision of his future aspirations justify Jawaharlal Nehru's statement that "Gokhale was considered one of the Elder Statesmen even when he was in his late thirties."[21] The political situation in India was at that time so tense, almost so desperate, as to test even Gokhale's statesmanship to its last limit. To start with, there was the impending visit of the

Prince of Wales. The country, and especially Bengal, was in no mood to come out with declarations of loyalty and welcome. On the other hand, the cause of securing Indian political reform through an Act of the British Parliament was not likely to be helped by an attitude either of sullenness or of hostility towards a representative of the British Crown. Gokhale had the insight and the courage to state that the Crown in the British Constitution is above party politics of the Government of the day. The King represents the permanent non-partisan elements of British policy, such as are reflected in the Queen's Proclamation, which was a charter of India's rights to freedom and equality within the Empire. In welcoming the Prince, the people of India were expressing their loyalty to the fountain of these cherished ideals of British rule in India.

While Gokhale had a series of hard things to say about Lord Curzon's administration, he had also to be fair to the now incumbent of the office of the Viceroy, Lord Minto. There was no reason to judge him before he had an opportunity to initiate his own policy. In anything that he did to retrace the repressive measures and other undesirable features of his predecessor's rule, the Viceroy was entitled to have the fullest cooperation of the Indian people. Lord Minto himself could ask for no more. This attitude of reciprocal conciliation adopted by Gokhale in his Presidential speech, and thereafter, went a long way in creating a bridge between him and the other Congress leaders on the one hand, and the new Viceroy and the new Government of His Majesty at Home, represented by the Liberal Cabinet of Campbell-Bannerman, on the other. The prolonged negotiations about reform which had to progress through the changing vicissitudes of Indian and British politics could not have been brought to a constructive and fruitful end in the absence of an atmosphere of responsive cooperation created for the new representative of the Crown who succeeded Lord Curzon.

For Curzon, as a devoted and capable administrator, Gokhale had great regard. But as a representative of the British Crown, sent to direct the Government of India according to the terms of the Proclamation and the several Parliamentary enactments, no worse choice could be imagined. Curzon had no respect either for the people of India or for their culture. He mistrusted their loyalty and their competence. He suppressed with vigour even the natural outlet to free expression or free civic organization of the people. By the time he left the shores of India, frustration of all the politically-minded people in the country and their estrangement from the bureaucratic rulers was so extreme, especially over the partition of Bengal, that Gokhale felt constrained, to observe :

If all Indians are to be treated as no better than dumb-driven cattle; if men, whom any other country would delight to honour are to be thus made to realize the utter humiliation and helplessness of their position in their own, then all I can say is: "Good-bye to all hope of cooperating in anyway with the bureaucracy in the interest of the people." I can conceive of no graver indictment of British rule in India than that such a state of things should be possible after a hundred years of that rule.[22]

Gokhale had very much at heart the cause of Indian industrialization and he wholeheartedly approved of the creed of *Swadeshi* as a policy of voluntary protectionism. He had also approved and appreciated the political results of the boycott movement in Bengal. In principle for a similar cause in similar circumstances he would not object to a general or prolonged boycott. Expatiating on this somewhat complex subject, he explains his position as follows: "This (boycott movement) they did with a two-fold object, first as a demonstration of their deep resentment at the treatment they were receiving, and secondly, to attract the attention of the people in England to their grievances, so that those who were in a position to call the Government of India to account might understand what was taking place in India. It was thus as a political weapon, used for a definite political purpose, that they had recourse to the boycott; and in the circumstances of their position they had every justification for the step they took. And I can tell you from personal experience that their action has proved immensely effective in drawing the attention of English people to the state of things in our country. But a weapon like this must be reserved only for extreme occasions. There are obvious risks involved in its failure and it cannot be used with sufficient effectiveness unless there is an extraordinary upheaval of popular feeling behind it."[23]

It is obvious that Gokhale had no ideological or conscientious objection to boycott as a political weapon. He felt that in the India of 1905, its general adoption was not warranted either by need or by feasibility. It is interesting to note that some leaders who then held very advanced positions on this subject demurred to Gandhi's non-cooperation movement in 1920 as too premature and too costly. This only shows that with great leaders of political, as of armed conflicts, judgments in the choice of strategy and weapons are apt to differ. It is only the issue of the struggle which renders *postfacto* validity to many a hazardous venture.

In his Presidential address, Gokhale minced no words in denouncing the evils of economic drain or blood-letting in a system of absentee capitalism, or of the dwarfing of a subject race under the autocratic rule of another. "The goal of the Congress," as he put it, "is that India should be governed in the interests of the Indians themselves, and that in course of time, a form of Government should be attained in this country similar to what exists in the self-governing colonies of the Empire."[24] While effective self-government is unequivocally demanded, as regards the form of government, Gokhale was not quite certain that any particular type then obtaining in British colonies could with advantage be bodily transferred to India. For instance, as he later on indicated in many of his speeches on reform, he was inclined to favour some constitutional checks on the omnipotence of the legislature. He had his own views also on the matter of group or indirect elections, and he would have favoured a much greater measure of regional decentralization of power than was normal in British colonies. A study of the German federal, and the French local, governments had influenced Gokhale's views on the internal structure of a self-governing state. The stage at which an overall view of a desirable and complete constitution for India could or need be taken was not reached while Gokhale lived. It is, however, important to record that beyond the principle of self-government within the Empire he made no commitment as regards the suitability to India of any other feature of the British or of the colonial system of Government.

While invoking the authority of Gladstone's dictum: "It is liberty alone which fits men for liberty. This proposition like every other in politics, has its bounds, but it is far safer than the counter doctrine, wait till they are fit." Gokhale felt that there is a definite advantage in a gradual, rather than sudden or cataclysmic, transformation from an autocratic to a democratic way of living: "...for it is a reasonable proposition that the sense of responsibility required for the proper exercise of the political institutions of the West can be acquired by an Eastern people through practical training and experiment only."[25] No question of ethics or of the bona fide desire of British Parliament to grant powers of self-government is raised in this context. Later experience in India, and in other countries attaining independence through several ways, fully indicates the advantage of gradualism favoured by Gokhale. From another angle, it is significant to note that a new regime tends to be sustained by the means through which it is brought into being. On this subject, at a later stage Gandhi has made his position clear in similar terms. "It is true we cannot rise till our political condition is reformed. But not true that we should be able to progress if our political condition undergoes a change by any means and in any manner."[26] Gokhale had an obvious ideological and emotional commitment to Morley. He hoped for noticeable progress of Indian political reforms during latter's tenure of office as Secretary of State in the Liberal Cabinet. He owned to some pessimism as to the influence which the obstrutionist bureaucracy may exercise on Morley's progressive intentions. All these somewhat conflicting thoughts are best expressed in his own words:

"The new Prime Minister (Campbell-Bannerman) is a tried and trusted friend of freedom. And as regards the new Secretary of State for India what shall I say ? Large numbers of educated men in this country feel towards Mr. Morley as towards a Master, and the heart hopes and, yet trembles, as it had never hoped or trembled before. He, the reverent student of Burke, the disciple of Mill, the friend and biographer of Gladstone—will he courageously apply their principles and his own to the Government of the country, or will he too succumb to the influences of the India Office around him, and thus cast a cruel blight on hopes, which his own writings have done so much to foster?"[27]

Gokhale was so conscious of the difficulties that lay in the way of India's progress to freedom that he emphasised the moral, more than the substantive advantage of a popular struggle. "The real moral interest of a struggle," he said, "such as we are engaged in, lies not so much in the particular readjustment of present institutions which we may succeed in securing, as in the strength that the conflict brings us to be a permanent part of ourselves. The whole life of a people, which is broader and deeper than what is touched by purely political institutions is enriched even by failures, provided the effort has been all that it should be. For such enrichment the present struggle is invaluable."[28]

Exalted, as this moral optimism was, it would have left the large audience of Congressmen somewhat cold, had Gokhale not added a peroration in which he invoked Ranade's prophetic words:

"With a liberated manhood, with buoyant hope, with a faith that never shirks duty, with a sense of justice that deals fairly by all, with unclouded intellect and powers fully cultivated, and lastly, with a love that overleaps all bounds, renovated India will take her proper rank among the nations of the world, and be the master of the situation and of her own destiny."[29]

Crucial Five Years

The quinquennium which followed the Banaras session of the Congress was one of the most crucial and significant in the political history of India. Following on the partition of Bengal, and the wave of a resurgent anti-feeling originating from the Japanese victory over Russia, all types of intensive political activity was spreading in the country. The prestige of the Westerner was shaken and verbal as well as physical challenges to its pretensions were freely offered. A number of organizations, not strictly limited to political objectives, were started with a strong revivalist trend. Within existing political bodies such as the Congress, a vigorous challenge was being offered to the old leadership represented by Gokhale which was accused of being over trustful and not sufficiently enterprising. Gokhale fully sympathized with the ultimate objective of national freedom, and he was not too sure that even if Morley did agree to move as far and as fast as Gokhale desired, the influences surrounding him in England and in India would allow him to do so. Gokhale, however, felt that considering the stage at which general political education and consciousness of the Indian people were, it was desirable, as the next step, to get out of the new British Government as full a measure of advance as possible. By using the new opportunities to consolidate our position and to equip ourselves to take a longer stop in future, he thought we would be acting in the best interests of the country.

In any case, so far as he himself was concerned, Gokhale felt that to back Morley in his progressive and liberal measures, and to influence their formulation to the best of his opportunities was the most positive contribution which 'he could then make to the progress of the nation. Friends of India in England had realized that Gokhale's appeal to the initially well-inclined section of the British public was a valuable asset in securing parliamentary support for progressive policies in India. It was in response to such a feeling that during 1906 Gokhale undertook two journeys to England. Morley's firm refusal to support the high-handed measures of the Lieutenant-Governor of East Bengal had raised a veritable storm against him. By his speeches in London on the state of things in the East Bengal, Gokhale was able to convey to the British public the flagrantly un-British nature of Fuller's rule in East Bengal. Even elementary rights of citizenship such as those of education, free speech, and public meetings were peremptorily violated, sometimes by more executive action. There was no prospect of local feeling being pacified so long as this state of things continued. The reactions of the East Bengal situation on the rest of the country were also most undesirable. The good intentions of the British people and the promises made in their solemn declarations had to be vindicated by suitable action. Gokhale felt that nothing short of a removal of the Left. Governor from the scene or his high-handed actions would meet the requirements of the case. Morley persisted in his firm refusal to back Fuller, and the latter eventually resigned. Fuller's discomfiture came as a reassuring factor in all otherwise gloomy situation.[30] But the Anglo-Indian bureaucracy never forgave either Morley or Gokhale for the part which they had played. In their own way both continued to draw on themselves the full measure of open and concealed opposition from official quarters in India to all measures designed to recognize the claim of Indians to equality and to freedom.

For the part played by Gokhale in representing to the British public India's case on several subjects of national importance, he was thanked by a formal resolution moved at the Congress session held in Calcutta at the end of year (1906). In acknowledging this outstanding mark of grateful appreciation of his fellow-workers, Gokhale emphatically called upon them to treat Morley's efforts at liberalizing the Indian government with sympathetic appreciation and to lend to them maximum co-operation. He again made it clear that the actual extent of these reforms may not be all that they desired, but it was only by accepting them and working them in the spirit in which they were offered that advance to further more liberal stages would be facilitated. Throughout this period almost all of the public speeches of Gokhale addressed to his countrymen contained a strong plea for appreciative co-operation with the new Secretary of State to liberalize and popularize the system of government in India.

REFERENCES

1. Nanda, B.R., *Gokhale, op. cit.*, p. 62.
2. *Speeches and Writings of Gopal Krishna Gokhale* (New York: Asia Publishing House), 1966, pp. 137-40.
3. *Ibid.*, p. 144.
4. *Ibid.*, pp. 149-156.
5. Quaterly Journal of *The Poorna Sarvajanik Sabha*, January 1894.
6. Nanda, B.R., *Three Statesmen: Gokhale, Gandhi and Nehru, op. cit.*, pp. 112-13.
7. *Speeches and Writings of Gopal Krishna Gokhale, op. cit.*, pp. 115-34.
8. *Ibid.*
9. *Ibid.*, pp. 5-17.
10. *Ibid.*
11. *Ibid.*, pp. 173-80.
12. Gandhi, M.K., *An Autobiography or The Story of My Experiments With Truth* (Ahmedabad: Navajivan Publishing House), 1942, p. 537.
13. *Speeches and Writings of Gopal Krishna Gokhale, op. cit.*, pp. 173-80.
14. Nehru, Jawaharlal, *Discovery of India* (Calcutta: Signet Press), 1948, p. 239.
15. Gandhi, M.K., *Constructive Programme: Its Meaning ansd Scope* (Ahmedabad: Navajivan Publishing House), 1952.

16. *Speeches and Writings of Gopal Krishna Gokhale, op. cit.*, pp. 321-25.
17. *Ibid.*, pp. 350-57.
18. *Ibid.*
19. *Ibid.*
20. *Ibid.*, pp. 333-39.
21. Nehru, Jawaharlal, *Autobiography* (London: The Bodley Head), 1947.
22. *Speeches and Writings of Gopal Krishna Gokhale, op. cit.*, Introduction, p. xxv.
23. *Ibid.*
24. Zaidi, A.M. and Others, *The Encyclopaedia of Indian National Congress*, Vol. IV, 1901-1905, op. cit., pp. 685-712.
25. *Ibid.*
26. Gandhi, M.K., *Gokhale – My Political Guru* (Ahmedabad: Navajivan Publishing House), 1952, p. 50.
27. *Speeches and Writings of Gopal Krishna Gokhale, op. cit.*, Introduction, p. xxvii.
28. *Ibid.*
29. *Ibid.*
30. *Ibid.*, pp. 364-367.

3

REFORMS AND POLITICAL AGITATION

Early in 1907, Gokhale addressed two important public meetings, one in Allahabad and the other in Lucknow. The former meeting was presided over by Motilal Nehru. Gokhale in his address said that the new century had opened with a new consciousness of hope and strength in the East, and even Lord Curzon's administration had been a blessing in disguise as it had helped to rouse the political consciousness of the people. In the course of his remarks, Gokhale clarified his own position on several important questions of political objectives and methods. As regards the goal to be reached by patriotic efforts of workers he observed:

"I recognize no limits to my aspiration for our motherland. I want our people to be in their own country what other people are in theirs. I want our men and women without distinction of caste or creed to have opportunities to grow to the full height of their stature unhampered by cramping and unnatural restrictions. I want India to take her proper place among the great nations of the world, politically, industrially, in religion, in literature, in science and in arts. I want all this and feel at the same time that the whole of this aspiration, in its essence and its reality, will be realized within this Empire."[1]

The whole concept of constitutional agitation was subjected to an analytical review and Gokhale stated his choice of methods in the following terms: "What were the methods they were entitled to employ? The first idea suggested was that physical force was excluded. Proceeding with the consideration further, three things were excluded: rebellion, aiding or abetting a foreign invasion, and resort to crime. Roughly speaking, barring these three things, all else was constitutional. No doubt everything that was constitutional was not necessarily wise or expedient. Prayers and appeals to justice lay at one end. Passive resistance, including even its extreme form of non-payment of taxes till redress was obtained, lay at the other end."

On the subject of wisdom or expediency of any particular method, at a given moment, opinions may differ. In particular, any suggestion of a complete dissociation from governmental organization was unacceptable to Gokhale. As he put it: "...the idea that they should leave the authorities severely alone and seek to attain their goal independently of them was inadmissible."

That the bureaucracy would generally be hostile to reforms was only to be expected. A sudden or cataclysmic change, even if it could be brought about, was not the best way to ensure their progress through conflicting claims and unfamiliar lines of organization. Above everything else he exhorted his countrymen not to be impatient and not to be deterred by only small gains and frequent failures.

"Nation-building is nowhere an easy task. In India it is beset with difficulties which are truly formidable and which will tax to the uttermost all our resources and all our devotion. Let us not forget that we are at a stage of the country's progress when our achievements are bound to be small, and our disappointments frequent and trying. That is the place which it has pleased Providence to assign to us in this struggle, and out responsibility is ended when we have done the work which belongs to that place. It will, no doubt, be given to our countrymen of future generations to serve India by their successes. We, of the present generation, must be content to serve her mainly by our failures."[2]

The speech at Lucknow which followed within a week was devoted largely to the *Swadeshi* movement. As a method of a kind of voluntary protection to national industries, Gokhale welcomed the movement. His understanding of the basic interdependence of nations, even under a regime of protectionism was, however, too sound to make him a supporter of a general boycott of foreign goods. Even in this speech, however, Gokhale's mind was really on the coming reforms, and the possible emergence within the Congress of a feeling of impatience and dissatisfaction with them. He tried to minimize this possibility by telling the audience:

"In the struggle that lies before us, we must be prepared for repeated disappointments. We must make up out minds that our progress is bound to be slow, and our successes in the beginning at any rate, comparatively small. But if we go to work with firm faith in our hearts, no difficulties can obstruct our way for long, and the future will be more and more on our side. After all, the industrial problem, formidable as it is, is not more formidable than the political problem."[3]

At this stage Gokhale was really in a very difficult position. The obstructionist and repressive bureaucracy in India was doing all it could to drive patriotic Indians, especially the educated youth, to a position of extreme opposition. The impact of this growing volume of resentment on the more aggressive and recalcitrant groups within the Congress was bound to cause a serious rift in that body. On the other hand Morley had either not the courage, or indeed the effective political power, to arrest the growth of intolerance and opposition among the ranks of the bureaucracy in India. The measure of reform which both Morley and Minto, especially the latter, proposed was so meagre that even in the most favourable circumstances effective control of Governmental power would continue to remain with the foreign bureaucracy. Even Gokhale could not be so optimistic as to hope that the reforms, if and when they came, would extend to sharing executive power of government with representative Indians. In these circumstances little was left for Gokhale to do beyond exhorting his countrymen to patience and to constructive co-operation and to press on the British authorities the need of a very early and a very large measure of political reform. In doing this he earned the immediate disfavour both of his countrymen and of the main British architects of the impending reforms, Morely and Minto.

Morely and Minto Reforms

Both Morley and Minto were convinced that the political relations with India and the form of its administration were unnatural. Lord Morley in a communication to Minto hoped that "If we can hatch out some plan and policy for a half a generation, that will be something, and if for a whole generation, that would be better. Only I am bent, as you assuredly are, on doing nothing to loosen the bolts." Minto, if anything, was moving even more slowly and reluctantly. Regarding Gokhale's prodding in respect of political reform, he observes: "Gokhale was very interesting and, I thought fair. The whole thing is a tremendous problem and there is a dead wall of official resistance always ready to obstruct anything which can be twisted into meaning interference with British official rights." Writing to Morley, Minto admits that "the more I see, the more convinced I am that we cannot continue to govern India with any hope of tranquility until we give her educated classes a chance of a greater share in the government of the country."[4] And yet both Minto and Morley spoke in terms of unmitigated disapproval of Gokhale's insistence on the rights of Indian leaders to conduct a peaceful agitation and on the need, so to enlarge the scope of reforms as to meet the demands of at least the more reasonable among the Indian leaders.

On the subject of Lala Lajpat Rai's deportation without trial, Gokhale had entered a strong protest. Referring to this, Minto writes to Morley:

"As to Gokhale, if he chooses to play with fire he must take the consequences. We can't afford to let him tamper with the Army, and if he says anything to me as to what has occurred, I shall tell him straight to his face. I am thoroughly disappointed by Gokhale; I had liked what I had seen of him and believed that he was honest at heart, but the part he has played of late has disgusted me. As an honest moderate he has lost a great opportunity of discountenancing rank sedition and what you tell me of his references to your speech shows either that lie is incapable of understanding the real friends of India or that he is, as you say, as big a revolutionist as Lajpat and the rest of them."[5]

Within three months of his having penned this petulent communication to Morley:

"As to Lajpat Rai and Ajit Singh, I have not a shadow of doubt that we must in common justice release them, and that the sooner we do so, the better. Now that we have declared the Punjab to be quiet, we cannot logically justify their farther imprisonment."[6]

Morley on his part felt hurt that Gokhale, instead of taking the opportunity to compromise with the British Government and accept the partial concession to his demands, was still pressing for further reforms to avoid a split among Indian leaders of the Congress. Instead of recognizing the patriotism and love of justice and fairness on the part of Gokhale, Morley accused him of merely being an inept politician. In a communication to Minto, he says:

"One of the most interesting things that have come in my way this week is a letter from Gokhale dated October 11, 1907. The one absorbing question, he says, is how the split in Congress, now apparently inevitable, is to be averted. I have often thought during the last twelve months that Gokhale, as a party manager, is a baby. Now, if I were in Gokhale's shoes I should insist on quietly making terms with the bureaucracy on the basis of Order plus Reform. If he would have the sense to see what is to be gained by this line, the 'split' when it comes should do him no harm, because it would set him free to fix his aims on reasonable things, where he might get out of us sixty or seventy per cent of what he might ask for."[7]

Thus, when put to the test, even Morley, whom Gokhale looked upon as a Master, expected him to make terms with the bureaucracy on a sixty per cent basis, forgetting his aim and willingly forsaking his comrades for his official allies! Had Gokhale been no more than a partisan or a factious politician, probably he would have made himself personally more acceptable to the Secretary of State and to the bureaucracy. His standing out for the liberties of colleagues, with whom he did not always see eye to eye on every thing, or his exerting himself to keep the Congress united by pressing on the British Government the need and the justice of larger reform measures was not to the liking of their lordships. On the other hand, his opponents in the Congress accused him of too much of a compromising spirit and of deliberately working to undo the more advance positions reached at the Calcutta Congress. In the correspondence which he published in a Calcutta paper on the subject of the debacle at the Surat session of the Congress, the soundness and at the same time the difficulties of his position as an honest servant of the Congress and of India are fully revealed.

Lala Lajpat Rai

It was on this incident, the deportation of Lajpat Rai and the persecution the other leaders of the Punjab without even the shred of any evidence of wrong-doing on their part, that Gokhale based his strong attack on a Bill to authorize prevention of meetings likely to promote sedition or to cause a disturbance of public tranquility:

"That a man like Lala Lajpat Rai, loved by thousands not in his province only, a man of high character and of elevated feeling, a keen religious and social reformer, and a political worker who, whatever his faults, worked only in broad daylight, should have been suddenly arrested and deported without a trial—this was a proceeding which stunned the people throughout India. And as regards the Rawalpindi case, what shall I say! For four months the whole country witnessed the spectacle of the venerable—Lala-Hansraj, a man as incapable of promoting disorder as any member sitting at this table—with other gentlemen equally respectable, rotting in the lock-up on a charge of inciting to violence and conspiring against the Crown! It will be long before the memory of the suffering of these men is wiped from the public mind. Meanwhile the country is waiting to see how the authorities deal with those who brought these sufferings on them by producing evidence which the trying Magistrate has pronounced to be most untrustworthy, and probably fabricated! With these things happening in the country, is it any wonder that the voice of those who counsel patience and moderation and self-restraint should be for the time at a discount among their countrymen? The occurrences of the last six months have afforded ample encouragement to those who like to talk strongly and do not occasionally talk wildly."[8]

He again reminded the Viceroy and the other Councillors that when one speaks of Loyalty in India he speaks not of a sentiment similar to that of feudal Europe or of Rajput India, but of a feeling of attachment to British rule and of a desire for its stability based on enlightened self-interest, on an appreciation of what the rule has on the whole done for the people in the past and of the conditions which it ensures for future progress. In spite of Gokhale's reasoned opposition, this Bill was put on the statute book. When the Act came for a renewal at the end of three years Gokhale recalled his opposition to the original Act, which he described as a Draconian piece of legislation. He supported the description by reference to a case in East Bengal in which members of a local community were proceeded against under the Act for meeting to consider what steps they should take to meet the situation created by a strike of barbers.

Decentralization and Dcmocracy

While attending to the best of his ability to urgent problems created either by his more ebullient colleagues in the Congress or by the determined official opponents of equality and freedom, during proceedings in the Council, Gokhale was doing all he could to activate, accelerate and broaden the course of British official policy of liberalization and democratization of governmental machinery in India. The note which he submitted to the Royal Commission on Decentralization emphasized two points of basic significance for the evolution of a federal democracy. The officials' interest in decentralization was confined to seeking more powers of independent action for the Provincial Governments. Gokhale felt convinced that unless this process of official decentralization was simultaneously accompanied by a measure of popularization of the provincial governments they would only emerge as "little despotisms." They would be a greater source of local tyranny or high-handedness than the system under which a Central Government for all India has to decide a policy before it can have effect anywhere in the country. Gokhale stood for a substantial provincialization of all internal administration on condition, however, that the Provincial Governments were suitably democratized. Gokhale's preference for decentralization with democracy did not stop at the provincial stage. He desired and recommended, that District Administration also should be decentralized and democratized in two ways. Functions which could be left to the District Local Boards should be administered by those bodies, and their composition should be progressively popularized...Functions, which continue to be the responsibility of the District Collector or Commissioner as representative of the Provincial Government should be administered by him, in consultation with an Advisory Council, which also should be increasingly democratized. This proposal about the District Boards and Councils sought to give effect to a plan of all-round local self-government through elected bodies adumbrated by Ranade. In almost every speech or writing of Gokhale on the subject of Governmental reform, this part of constitutional reorganization is given a prominent place. He was aware of the most obvious objection on the score of avoidable duplication of bodies. This he sought to meet by a further proposal to broaden, at an appropriate stage, the functions of a fully democratized District Board so as to include certain advisory responsibilities and rights concerning provincial administration within the district as well.

Order with Reform

Morley's prescription for India, Order with Reform, which he tried unsuccessfully to "sell" to Gokhale was administered nonetheless during 1908 with vigour. By a ruthless exercise of authority both under the ordinary and extraordinary criminal law, a veritable reign of terror was let loose in the country. It was the belief of the Viceroy and his Anglo-Indian advisers, that unless special powers of coercion were vested in Government, the life and property of Europeans were not safe. They were persuaded further to believe that unless the European population in India was so reassured they may take the law into their own hands and a civic disaster would follow. Considering the relative positions of the armed strength of the Government and the utter helplessness of a completely disarmed people, this cry of Europeans in danger was nothing but a bureaucratic ruse to soften the Viceroy's and especially the Secretary of State's enthusiasm for reform. While Minto recognized the need to incorporate into government some elements from among loyal Indians, his actual programme to give effect to this policy was both elementary and crude. He appears to have favoured a Council of Notables, or of Nabobs as Morley put it. This body of about sixty completely nominated members was to act in a purely advisory capacity. When Minto found that his proposal did not evoke favourable reception, he suggested a small expansion of councils, with official and nominated majorities. In fact he preferred to continue the earlier system of having a confirmatory stage of nomination even after preliminary elections for the "elected" seats had taken place. Minto had quite a number of advisers who held that the Indian Government was the inheritor of the absolute powers of the Great Moghul and what the British Parliament expects its representatives in India to do was to give this despotism a constitutional procedure. Morely did not countenance these constructions and suggestions. For him a progressive democratization was the only course which events in India could legitimately take, though he would try his best to steady the course as much as possible.

In fairness to Morley it must be recognized that in addition to the powerful obstacle of the European and official blocks in India, the non-official public opinion in England, even in the Liberal party, had not been sufficiently educated and oriented in respect of Indian self-government. What Gokhale was doing in this direction, in India as well as in England, was, therefore, of the utmost value for the success of even the limited plans which Morely envisaged. Reactionary officials occasionally expressed strong resentment against the close contacts maintained by Morley, and to a certain extent also by Minto, with Gokhale. Speaking of one such attempt, Morley wrote to Minto: "I have an invincible faith in what Mathew Arnold called 'sweet reasonableness.' Sir Charles Elliott, former Lft. Governor of Bengal, abhored the idea of holding any communion with Gokhale until he had openly and formally denounced the extremist press. As if it were of no importance or advantage to us to be on terms with men like Gokhale!"[9] Minto, who had more normal and frequent occasions to meet Gokhale, however, never ceased to regret that certain members of the British Parliament allowed themselves to be influenced more by men like Gokhale than by men on the spot, that is, by the Viceroy and the bureaucracy.

Mohamedan Representation

A very glaring case of misunderstanding arose in connection with a note on reforms submitted to Morley in September, 1908. The broad outlines of this note were in keeping with Gokhale's ideas on the subject to which he had given public expression on several occasions. An expansion of the Central and Provincial Councils by elected majority in the latter, and non-official majority in the former, inclusion of Indians in Executive Councils, powers of discussion and of moving of resolutions on the budget, right of moving resolutions on all items of public importance, provision of a veto to the Governors in provincial, and to the Governor-General in both central and provincial matters, and a reform of the district administration, were some of the important features of Gokhale's own proposals. On the question of separate elections for Mohamedans, a point of agreement had not been reached. Gokhale's personal view on the subject was, as he had made clear, on several occasions, that elections should be held by the general body of voters for all the elective seats. If any strong sense of exclusion existed among the Mohamedan voters because of their having been able to put into the legislature a smaller number of members than what by their proportionate strength in the population they were entitled to, supplementary elections for the requisite number of seats should be held through the voters of that community. Such an arrangement was feasible in the immediate context, as a certain number of nominated seats were still available. Moreover, as the role of the legislators was to be only a representative and largely advisory one, a few numbers on one side or the other did not matter. It appears that initially the Government of India was favourable to this idea, but Morley in presenting his proposals to Parliament outlined a new scheme of his own which bore no resemblance to Gokhale's ideas. Some critics of his felt this to be an evidence of what they called Hindu Intrigue in London. It was to repudiate this insinuation that Gokhale had to explain the full circumstances in a letter to *The Times*.[10]

It appears, however, that Gokhale's position on communal electorates continued to be misinterpreted here as well as in England. In a speech in Marathi delivered on behalf of the Deccan Sabha, he addressed himself directly to the Hindu-Mohamedan question. Like so many Indian leaders, before and after him, he was convinced that without communal unity a stable progressive national State could not be established. Equally well in the atmosphere of common subjection to an alien rule the prospect of all-round realization of this truth appeared to be dim. The past history of India was of little direct help in an early forging of bonds of communal unity against such odds. Taking all these circumstances into account, Gokhale has given an overall assessment of the subject in this important speech:

"Over the greater part of India the two communities had inherited a tradition of antagonism, which, though it might ordinarily lie dormant, broke forth into activity at the smallest provocation. The tradition which had to be overcome by spread of education, a wide and efficient performance of civic duties, growth of national aspirations and a quickening of national self-respect in both communities, were among the forces which would ultimately overcome the tradition.

In the best interest of their public life and for the future of their land, they must first have elections on a territorial basis in which all communities without distinction of race or creed should participate and then special supplementary elections should be held to secure the fair and adequate representation of such important minorities as had received less than their full share in the general elections.

The Government of India's original proposals had been very much on these lines; proportionate representation for the Mohamedans, partly through general, and partly through special electorates. The Secretary of State, however, having proposed from the highest motives, as they could all see, a scheme of his own and having afterwards found it necessary to abandon it and fall back on the Government of India's proposals, did so in language which opened the door to large demands by the Moslem League.

When any one urged that his community was specially important and should, therefore, receive representation in excess of its fair share, the undoubted and irresistible implication was that the other communities were comparatively inferior and should receive less than their fair share. That was a position to which naturally the other communities could not assent."[11]

Legislative Reform

Representation of minorities was only one among several important aspects of constitutional reform in which Gokhale failed to carry conviction either to the Government of India or to the Secretary of State. In his note submitted to Morley, Gokhale, had urged the formation of budget committees of the legislature, both at the centre and in the provinces. His own experience of budget discussions had convinced him by then that speeches made by a few members on the non-official side after a budget is formally presented by Government is not the best way to seek to influence budgetary action in the interests of the people. If while the budget is in the process of preparation, and in any case before it is put to the vote, non-official representatives could sit with the officials and discuss their views on policy as well as its implementation in detail, the extent and timeliness of non-official influence may be enhanced. Incidentally, this procedure that that may help to train non-official members in the responsibilities connected with public revenue and expenditure did not find it easy to persuade his colleagues to co-operate towards a scheme of reforms with which he himself was in complete agreement. Speaking on the subject at the (1908) Madras session of the Congress, he explained why he thought that in spite of the limitations of the scheme, a policy of grateful appreciation was justified.[12] Taking the reform of the Councils and the further reforms which may come as a result of the Decentralization Commission together, he felt that a substantial advance would be made. It was, in his opinion, not reasonable at that stage of the progress of our national movement to expect effective control over either legislation or administration. He felt, however, that the new reforms provided for what he called "responsive association from within." This would ensure preventive influence over undesirable legislation. A constant attitude of antagonism would produce no constructive results. Even the ultimate veto of the Governor-General could be rendered ineffective by a tradition of responsible association among official and non-official members. In this respect the appointment of Indian members to the Secretary of State's Council, and to the Executive Councils of the Viceroy and Governors had a special relevance. Further progress towards a fuller sharing of powers can only be made through a wholehearted and competent discharge of the limited responsibilities and powers conferred on them.

Indians in South Africa

During these eventful years there was only one subject for which Gokhale allowed his concentration on Reforms to be partially diverted. That subject was the one for which he held himself almost completely at the disposal of Gandhi to act in support of Indians in South Africa. In a public meeting held in Bombay in September, 1909, Gokhale regretted that racial discrimination against Indians should continue to be imposed in a Crown Colony, Transvaal, in spite of the strong opinion expressed against it both in India and in South Africa. He wholeheartedly supported Gandhi in his stand, and in particular in his campaign of passive resistance, against which so much criticism was offered, even by some of his usual supporters. The following passage from Gokhale's speech brings out his complete understanding with Gandhi, and, what is more significant is his acceptance of passive resistance when all other means have proved ineffective.

"In fighting for the principle that no humiliating disabilities shall be imposed by the statute book of a British Colony on Indians as Indians, Mr. Gandhi is fighting for the assertion of our claim to that equality with which our hopes for the future are bound up. I have heard it said by some friends, mainly Englishmen, that though they originally sympathized with the Indians in this struggle, Mr. Gandhi's resort to Passive Resistance, involving as it does defiance of the laws of the Colony, has alienated their sympathies. Now I do not in the first place think that this is a fact, for we see the Committee in England, presided over by Lord Ampthill, backing up the passive resisters as strongly and as cordially as ever. Again, even if a few Englishmen have grown cold in their sympathies, I am sure none of us here feels anything but the highest admiration for the manner in which the struggle has been carried on by our side. I think, and I say this deliberately, that in the circumstances of the Transvaal, Passive Resistance, such as that organized by Mr. Gandhi, is not only legitimate, but is a duty testing on all self-respecting persons. What is this Passive Resistance? Passive Resistance to an unjust law or an oppressive measure is a refusal to acquiesce to that law or measure and a readiness to suffer the penalty... If we strongly and clearly and conscientiously feel the grave injustice of law, and there is no other way to obtain redress, I think refusal to acquiesce to it, taking the consequences of such refusal, is the only course left to those who place conscience and self-respect above their material and immediate interests."[13]

On the South African question Gokhale and Gandhi agreed that the issue and the time both justified resort to Passive Resistance. It is conceivable that he may not have agreed either with Gandhi or some one else as to the propriety of adopting Passive Resistance in respect of some other issue or at some other time. But that in Gokhale's armoury of the weapons of constitutional agitation' Passive Resistance occupied a place reserved for readily usable items cannot be denied. The moral which Gokhale drew from the plight of Indians in South Africa was :

"The root of our present troubles in the colonies really lies in the fact that our status is not what it should be in our own country. Men, who have no satisfactory status in their own land, cannot expect to have satisfactory status elsewhere."[14]

Passive Resistance

That Gokhale's acceptance of passive resistance as a legitimate method of a citizen's political action in appropriate conditions was a conclusion arrived at after mature thought is further borne out by his remarks on the subject when the situation in Transvaal was under discussion at the Lahore Congress. Gokhale in moving for adoption of the relevant resolution said:

"Our appeal to our own countrymen is that a small colony in Transvaal is doing its duty in the matter (Improvement in the conditions of indentured labour). It has done nothing unworthy but everything worthy. It is engaged in what is known as the passive resistance struggle. What is the passive resistance struggle? It is essentially defensive in its nature and it fights with moral and spiritual weapons. A passive resister resists tyranny by undergoing suffering in his own person. He pits soul force against brute force; he pits the divine in man against the brute in man; he pits suffering against oppression; he pits conscience against might; he pits faith against injustice, right against wrong. A passive resister deliberately and openly violates the requirements of art, unjust law or order or the simple reason that he cannot conscientiously submit to that law or order. He does not seek to evade the consequences of that law but invites them and he glories in them. It is a spiritual struggle essentially in keeping with the highest traditions of Indian spirituality. I repeat that our countrymen have done nothing unworthy. On the contrary, everything that they have done is worthy of them."[15]

All through his active political life since 1899 Gokhale was tilting his lance of reason—be it in the shape of sweet reasonableness—against the armed insight, the brute force, of the bureaucracy. Even if he could he would not, as a civilized and conscientious human being, easily bring himself to pitting his own brute force against bureaucratic brute force. But by this time, his contact with Gandhi and the progress of the just struggle of Indian settlers in South Africa under the latter's leadership, had shown to him the existence of a political weapon even more potent than reason in dealing with brute force. The mass support, the discipline and sacrifice, and selfless yet competent leadership, such as that of Gandhi, may not be forthcoming on every issue, however just it may be. But if a vicious system refused to bend under normal pressure of political agitation, for Gokhale, " passive resistance is not only legitimate, but it is a duty."

Inevitability of Further Political Reform

Both by the way in which the Press Act was administered and by the attitude generally of officers towards the new changes brought about by the Morley Minto Reforms, Gokhale felt considerably disturbed. While he recognized the good intentions of both Morley and Minto, and also generally the conciliatory approach of the latter, he was frank in making his dissatisfaction with the actual implementation of reforms known to friends in India and in U.K. It was inferred that unless the scope of reforms was considerably enlarged so as to place the elected Indian element in a position of effective influence, and not merely of responsible association from within, the real purpose of the reforms and the needs of progressive government will not be met. Morley who knew Gokhale better and who had a broader background as a political philosopher was probably not surprised at Gokhale's frustrations at the actual results of the reforms.

But Viceroy Minto looked upon this attitude of Gokhale as worse than disappointing. On being informed by Morley of a letter written by Gokhale to a mutual friend in U.K. complaining about the generally hostile reaction to reforms on the part of Europeans and officials, Minto wrote back as follows:

"I am glad you sent me the extract from Gokhale's letter to his friend in England. It is very important as showing his hand, I am sorry to say. I can only call it mischievous, and written with the intention to mislead. Gokhale would not have spoken in the same sense to me. And that is the worst of him, that one cannot rely upon his absolute good faith. I know him well, admire him much, and am on most friendly terms with him, in ability and breadth of view he is a long way ahead of any Indian in political life. But he must know quite well that the picture he gave in his letter is not a true one. Our repressive measures are certainly not severe and the suggestion that they will be hardly used is unjustifiable. The tendency of Local Governments will be generally the other way. Then the suggestion that the official world is opposed to reforms and advance is quite untrue. There has been an extraordinary change in that direction. No doubt the reforms were originally unpopular generally with the bureaucracy, but the people who do not recognize their value now are very few and far between...But the worst symptom in what Gokhale writes is that he apparently does not mean to accept the Reforms with the goodwill which is so important for their success. If he goes on the lines of at once picking holes in it and asking for further alterations, he will make a great mistake in a patriotic sense. After all, Gokhale represents a very small minority in India but it is a dangerous minority in that undue weight is attached to its views."[16]

The British Parliamentary perspective of the Liberal statesman, Morely was, however, different from this Olympic pronouncement of the Viceroy of India. Morley, writing to Minto around the same time, revising the system of administration which the two had to work together for five years, observed:

"It is a terribly cumbrous and artificial sort of system, and I am not certain that it will last for ever, or even for many years to come. I suspect that you surmise the same."[17]

The period that followed the Reforms of 1909, was not a happy one for Gokhale. While he was prepared in good faith to accept small steps forward towards an accepted goal he was not content to swallow without a protest a malingering and disruptive attitude on the part of those who were charged with the responsibility of honest implementation of reform measures. As far as it was consistent with his essentially dedicated and hopeful outlook on his responsibilities towards the country, Gokhale felt continuously frustrated ever since. It was with great difficulty that he was trying to persuade the leaders, within and without the Congress, to work for the Reforms as an important step towards the realization of a higher nationhood. He received support for this appeal in the performance of officials, who in fact pursued their attempts at suppression of the political movement and at dividing the ranks of Indian politicians with even greater determination than before.

Enlightened Loyalty and Limited Co-operation

Within the Supreme Legislative Council itself, little improvement was visible in the Government's attitude towards legitimate political activity, the people and towards their political aspirations. The Press Act of 19 was followed by the Seditious Meeting Bill of 1911, intended to be on the Statute Book as a permanent measure. The speech which Gokhale made in opposing this measure is significant in two respects. He restated his position on the theme of loyalty to Government and clearly indicated the limits within which

Government in India were entitled to expect the co-operation of their subjects.

Just as the right of free speech is an abstract right so also the proposition that all loyal citizens must rally round, the executive in maintaining law and order is an abstract proposition, and its value as a guide to political conduct must depend upon the circumstances amidst which it is sought to be applied.

"And then, after a great deal of consideration, I have come to the conclusion that while things are as they are today, our co-operation with Government cannot ordinarily go beyond two classes of measures—constructive measures taken for the moral and material well-being of the people and measures urgently and immediately necessary to deal with actual or threatened disturbances."[18]

This mood of sullen dissatisfaction was further strengthened by happenings in South Africa. His emphasis on racial equality within the Empire, and his spiritual as well as political involvement in Gandhi's activities in the Transvaal occupied a much larger part of Gokhale's thinking than was or is generally recognized. His visit to South Africa in 1912, was a crucial event in the formulation, confirmation and progress of his political thinking. The parting appeal which he made to Indians in Pretoria on November 15, 1912 gives us an inkling of the sharpening of his reactions to the entrenched positions of the vested interests in the British Empire.

You have by no means in my position here, and it is not impossible that it may grow worse. But, whatever happens, do not lose faith or give way to despair. I pray to God that such a struggle as you found it necessary to wage in the Transvaal during the last three years may not have to be waged again. But if it has to be resumed, or if you have to enter struggles of a like nature for justice denied or injustice forced on you, remember that the issue will largely turn on the character you show, on your capacity for combined action, on your readiness to suffer and sacrifice in a just cause."[19]

Soon after his return from South Africa, Gokhale attended the annual session of the Congress held in Bankipur. Jawaharlal Nehru, who also was present, found that "Gokhale, fresh from South Africa, was the outstanding person of the session. He seemed to be one of the few persons present who took politics and public affairs seriously and felt deeply about them. I was impressed by him."[20]

The main interest in politics for Gokhale after this date lay mainly in organizing the political life of the country on stronger and more cohesive lines. The work within the legislature did not by any means exhaust his capacity to be of use to his countrymen. He had accepted membership of the Royal Commission on Public Services in India on account of his life-long interest in the process of Indianization. Largely owing to his failing health he was not able to do as much for the Commission as he would otherwise have done. In fact when he passed away in February 1915, this Commission had its report. He had, however, occasion, on account of this still to submit Commission twice to visit England. During these visits he was able on a more direct basis to exchange ideas with friends of India in that country on the need of an early advance of further political reform. Strength and unity of political life in India, and an active support for Indian self-government in U.K. were the two most engrossing interests of Gokhale during these years.

Post-War Reforms

The War, which commenced in August 1914, came as an altogether new factor in the situation. It soon became clear that not only tranquillity in India but its active and wholehearted support would be needed to help Great Britain and its allies to win ultimate success in the struggle. This realization was, however, gradual and in fact, it fluctuated with the fortunes of British arms from time to time. Early in the days of the War the full implications of its lasting effects were not known. Gokhale, who was nursing a serious ailment within himself, was under a special difficulty to appraise the full implications of the situation, internal and international and, to organize suitable action. It was mostly from his sick bed that he was attending as a matter of duty to all affairs, which came before him in the course of such a restricted routine. Towards the middle of January 1915 he was asked by Lord Willingdon, the then Governor of Bombay, to discuss with him the subject of further political reforms for India. So far as Lord Willingdon himself was concerned, the initiative with the Government of India was to be his own. To secure fuller Indian support to the War effort he felt that a declaration of further reforms was called for. Knowing the limitations of Lord Willingdon and having no more than the first six months of the War behind him, what he would be justified in suggesting to the authorities at Simla and London was the question. Due to illness, Gokhale could not succeed in arranging a meeting with two of his colleagues, Pherozeshah Mehta and the Aga Khan, whom he occasionally consulted on such matters. Being pressed by Willingdon, Gokhale pencilled a draft for his use. This was to have been discussed with Mehta and the Aga Khan before dispatch. Mehta did not obviously reply, and the Aga Khan only wrote back suggesting the addition of a clause regarding German East Africa, which he felt should be turned over to India after the War, for colonization by Indians.

This, however, proved to be the end of Gokhale's own activity in politics, as almost on the morrow of the dispatch of the draft, he breathed his last. It is important to note these circumstances attending the draft on post-war reforms in India to make it clear, firstly, that it did not represent Gokhale's own considered and complete views about a long term solution of India's constitutional needs, and, secondly, that it was in no sense a testament which he addressed to his own people. The draft contained a set of proposals which, in the opinion of Gokhale, Lord Willingdon could on his own press on the Government of India as a war measure. This draft would in all probability have remained buried in the official archives of Government, but for its publication by the Aga Khan in 1917, fully two years after it was first prepared. The Aga Khan was led on to do this because Jinnah earlier had, in his presidential address to the Provincial Conference held at Ahmedabad, outlined a scheme of Provincial autonomy which was strikingly similar to the contents of Gokhale's draft.

Organizing Freedom for Prosperity

If there is any such thing as a political testament of Gokhale for his people, it will have to be sought in no single one of his writings and speeches. In all his contributions from 1905, there are a number of basic concepts about a desirable political life for the people of this country. These concepts form a consistent whole of a broader life of freedom and prosperity which is the goal of political activity. Like all true lovers of freedom, Gokhale realized that important as politics is, it is by no means the only important thing in the legitimate interests of a civilized society. A variety of industrial, social and cultural associations freely and usefully operating in their respective spheres of interest must be considered to be equally necessary and important. For this reason an atmosphere and tradition of social equality and cultural freedom for all citizens in a community is essential to secure the maximum benefit out of a system of political equality and freedom. What Gokhale had to say about the evils of repression, and about the inherent value of freedom of association, meeting and expression, has universal and permanent validity.

All governments, irrespective of their outward forms, are tempted to assume executive powers over their subjects as a short-cut to easy suppression of all sources of opposition. The fact that these powers are conferred on the executive by the Legislatures of the day does not take away from the fact that executive restrictions narrow the base of that free association, among citizens on which the superstructure of constitutional government rests. Especially, if the controlling power in the legislature is held by a strong power group, which is for the time being securely entrenched, the risk of executive high-handedness covered with a legal cloak is all the greater. Freedom-loving citizens and their representatives have the duty to see that legal freedoms and ordinary processes of law are not denied to any citizen either by extraordinary legislation or by extraordinary procedures.

When Gokhale commenced his political life, not a single member of a Legislative Council was elected in the true sense of the word. An election had to be followed by a confirmatory nomination by Government. The number of even such members was almost negligible in a legislative body of the size of a modern cabinet in many State Governments, and much smaller than the number of ministers in the Central Government of India. The Morley-Minto Councils, which owed so much to the initiative and suggestion of Gokhale, were the last stage of political reform with which he was associated. Those councils lacked effective power either in the making or in the execution of laws. Except that the First World War, which had just commenced when he died, appeared to introduce a new unforeseen element in the situation, the power of Britain and its grip over dependent areas appeared to be unchallengeable. Against such a background Gokhale could concentrate only on small and immediate but necessary and difficult tasks. Even in these, more often than not, his generation could serve the country more by its failures than by its successes.

REFERENCES

1. *Speeches and Writings of Gopal Krishna Gokhale, op. cit.*, pp. 215-22.
2. *Ibid.*
3. *Ibid.*, pp. 223-35.
4. Minto, *Many Countries of India, Minto and Morley 1905-1910* (London: Macmillan), 1934, pp. 113, 161, 240.
5. *Ibid.*, p. 235-36.
6. *Ibid.*, p. 417
7. *Ibid.*
8. *Speeches and Writings of Gopal Krishna Gokhale, op. cit.*, pp. 18-36.
9. Minto, *Many Countries of Irdia, Minto and Morley 1905-1910, op. cit.*, footnote on p. xxxi.
10. *The Times*, London 19 April, 1909.
11. *Speeches and Writings of Gopal Krishna Gokhale, op. cit.*, pp. 307-12.
12. Zaidi, A.M. and Others, *The Encyclopaedia of Indian National Congress*, Vol. V, 1901-1905, op. cit., pp. 230-32.
13. *Speeches and Writings of Gopal Krishna Gokhale, op. cit.*, pp. 409-16.
14. *Ibid.*
15. *Ibid.*, pp. 417-25.
16. Minto, *Many Countries of India, Minto and Morley 1905-1910, op. cit.*, footnote p. xxxi.
17. *Ibid.*
18. *Speeches and Writings of Gopal Krishna Gokhale, op. cit.*, pp. 435-41.
19. *Ibid.*
20. Nehru, Jawaharlal, *Autobiography, op. cit.*, p. 27.

4

CONCEPT OF NATIONALISM

Gokhale took the pervious path of politics as a serious profession. He was a constructive statesman. His life of utter self-sacrifice and abnegation indicated that according to him nationalism was a species of self-devotion to a higher cause. For both Ranade and Gokhale, the basic task was the liberation of man by the development and enhancement of his moral, intellectual and physical abilities and talents. This vast ideal could be concretized through the adequate and dedicated harnessing of the energies of those who regarded themselves as servants of the people. This required that public duty and political work had to be viewed as pathways to consecrated national service. "Without suffering and a true spirit of comradeship and simplicity of life", Gokhale used to say, "nationalism could not become a living force." In his political tactics, he was a moderate and believed in constitutional agitation, The radical technique of boycott did not appeal to him. Like Burke, Gokhale believed in caution, slow evolution and rational progress. He was opposed to extreme measures and theatrical outbursts of popular frenzy.[1]

In a speech delivered in Poona in 1894, Gokhale acknowledged the contributions of the Indian National Congress to the task of nation-building. The forces that were earlier struggling in a scattered way for creating a strong solid nation had been sought to be united by the Congress[2] in such a way that, as a consequence, a common platform was available in the different parts of the country. Besides, supportive emotional response was also available in the different parts of the country to demands and issues of national welfare. The Congress had also made "public opinion in India more enlightened and more influential."[3] Furthermore, the Congress served as an Institutional mechanism through which pro-Indian British politicians could "do their duty by the people of the country."

Gokhale always had immense faith in British liberalism. He had trust in the English conscience. He always hoped, like Dadabhai, that a new English statesmanship, would arise, which would do justice to India. In his budget speech of 1902, he had said:

"What is needed is that we should be enabled to feel that we have a Government, national in spirit, though foreign in personnel—a Government which subordinates all other considerations to the welfare of the Indian people, which resents the indignities offered to Indians abroad as though they were offered to Englishmen and which endeavours by all means to further the moral and material interest of the people in India and outside India. The statesman who evokes such a feeling among the Indian people will render a great and glorious service to this country and will secure for himself an abiding place in the hearts of our people. Nay, he will do more—he will serve his own country in a true spirit of Imperialism—not the narrower Imperialism, which regards the world as though it was made for one race only and looks upon subject races as if they were intended to be mere footstools of that race but that nobler Imperialism which would enable all who are included in the Empire to share equally in its blessings and honours."[4]

Gokhale had sincere faith in the dawn of greater imagination in the English rulers which would enable them to perceive and value the sentiments that were pervading the educated Indian mind. Only such a psychological approach could prepare the foundations of "the fusion of Interest" between the British and the Indians. In the words of Motilal Nehru, G.K. Gokhale was the great apostle of self-government. He vehemently criticized the ruling bureaucracy for its gross irresponsibility and extreme callousness to public will in having effected the infamous partition of Bengal. He made emphatic protests against the harshness and oppressiveness of the bureaucracy. He urged upon the bureaucracy not to be satisfied with having acted up to the maxims of "efficiency" but so to govern India that Indians might be enabled to govern themselves according to the highest Western standards. He lamented the growing destitution of India under British rule, and also criticized the costly character of the administration of India by a foreign agency.

With his commitments to the philosophy of reason, spiritual and moral liberation and universal tolerance, Gokhale championed the cause of the "depressed classes". Speaking at the Dharwar Social Conference on April 27, 1903, he candidly confessed that the gospel of equality was a gift of the modern philosophy of enlightenment. The old civilizations had the stigma of social discrimination associated with them. He said:

"The classes of the West are a perfectly elastic institutions and not rigid or cast-iron like our castes. Mr. Chamberlain, who is the most masterful personage in the British Empire today, was at one time a shoemaker and then a screw maker. Of course, he did not make shoes himself, but that was the trade by which he made money. Mr. Chamberlain today dines with Royalty, and mixes with the highest in the land in terms of absolute equality. Will a shoe-maker ever be able to rise in India in the social scale in a similar fashion, no matter how gifted by nature he might be? A great writer has said that castes are eminently useful for the preservation of society, but that they are utterly unsuited for purpose of progress. And this I think is perfectly true. If you want to stand where you were a thousand years ago, the system of castes need not be modified in any material degree. If, however, you want to emerge out of the slough in which you have long remained sunk, it will not do for you to insist on a rigid adherence to caste. Modern civilization has accepted greater equality for all as its watchword, as against privilege and exclusiveness which were the root-ideas of the old world."[5]

Although Gokhale accepted the supremacy of the Paramount Power and believed in the blessings of British connexion, his mind and vision were lit with the panorama of a glorious future for India. In his budget speech of 1903, he said:

"The India of the future, will, under Providence, not be an India of diminishing plenty, of empty prospect, or of justifiable discontent; but one of expanding industry, of awakened faculties, of increasing prosperity, and of more widely distributed comfort and wealth. I have faith in the conscience and purpose of my own country, and I believe in the almost illimitable capacities of this. But under no other conditions can this future be realized than the unchallenged supremacy of the Paramount Power, and under no other controlling authority is this capable of being maintained than that of the British Crown."[6]

Gokhale believed in the harmonious co-operation of India and England and, therefore, he would appreciate the growth of spirit of mutual understanding. Hence, he also wanted to help in devising a comprehensive plan for the moral and material rehabilitation of the country. One important step in that direction would be the implementation of the Policy of equality of treatment promised in the Charter Act of 1833 and the proclamation of 1858. The transgression of the pledges given would certainly amount to the disappearance of one of the main bases of India's loyalty. India's destiny was to obtain an honoured place among the family of nations, and the glory of England would lie in having helped in that consummation. The exclusion of Indians from its posts of responsibility would result in the dwarfing of their personality and a diminution of their moral stature. Hence Gokhale pleaded for increasing Indian participation in government. Thought he criticized the evils of a bureaucratic concentration of power, he continued to have sincere faith in the good intentions of British statesmen so much so that even when Dadabhai Naoroji was disillusioned, Gokhale retained his trust and confidence in British statesmen. He even supported with all his heart the Indian Councils Act of 1909.

Gokhale's approach to contemporary problems was dictated by two key propositions. He believed in Ranade's theory that the British empire in India was in the scheme of divine dispensation and was meant to be of immense benefit to India. Secondly, he believed in creating the strong foundations of nationalism through hard work and sacrifice. He believed in national consolidation. He, therefore, accepted the necessity of increasing the social efficiency and enhancing the moral character of the people as prerequisites for national growth because nationalism demands a consecrated spirit.

"...the real moral interest of a struggle, such as we are engaged in, lies so much in the particular readjustments of present institutions which we may succeed in securing, as in the strength that the conflict brings us to be a permanent part of ourselves. The whole life of a people, which is broader and deeper than what is touched by purely political institutions, is enriched even by failure, provided the effort has been all that it should be."[7]

In order to give his work of morally-oriented national consolidation a permanent shape on June 12, 1905, Gokhale established the Servants of India Society. The constitution of the Society reveals the deep and noble idealism of the founder whose life was a record of suffering, sweat and sorrow. He wanted the concretization of the ideal of a united, strengthened and renovated India whose super-structure would be founded upon sacrifices, devotion and sustained work. The preamble of the constitution of the Society lays down:

"The Servants of India Society has been established to meet in some measure these requirements of the situation. Its members frankly accept the British connection, as ordained in the inscrutable dispensation of Providence for India's good self-government on the lines of English colonies, as their goal. The goal they recognize, cannot be attained without years of earnest and patient work and sacrifices worthy of the cause...One essential condition of success is that a sufficient number of our countrymen must now come forward to devote themselves to that cause in the spirit in which religious work is undertaken. Public life must be spiritualized...A fervent patriotism which rejoices at every opportunity of sacrifice for the motherland, a dauntless heart which refuses to be turned back from its object by difficulty or a danger, a deep faith in the purpose of Providence that nothing can shake—equipped with these, the worker must start on his mission and reverently seek the joy which comes of spending oneself in the service of one's country. The Servants of India Society will train men, prepared to devote their lives to the cause of the country in a religious spirit and will seek to promote, by all constitutional means, the national interests of the Indian people. Its members will direct their efforts principally forward: (i) creating among the people, by example and by precept, a deep and passionate love of the motherland, seeing its highest fulfilment in service and sacrifice, (ii) organizing the work of political education and agitation and strengthening the public life of the country, (iii) promoting relations of cordial goodwill co-operation among the different communities, (iv) assisting educational movements, especially those for the education of women, the education of backward classes, and industrial and scientific education, and (v) the elevation of the depressed classes."[8]

Gokhale supported the *Swadeshi* movement. To him *Swadeshi* meant an exalted, deep and all-embracing love of India. He said in his presidential speech at the Banaras Congress in 1905:

"... the true Swadeshi movement is both a patriotic and an economic movement. The idea of Swadeshi or 'one's own country' is one of the noblest conceptions that have ever stirred the heart of humanity. The devotion to motherland, which is enshrined in the boost Swadeshi, is an influence so profound and so passionate that its very thought thrills and its actual touch lifts one out of oneself. The Swadeshi movement, as it is ordinarily understood, presents one part of this gospel to the mass of our people in a form which brings it within their comprehension. It turns their thoughts to their country, accustoms them to the idea of voluntarily making some sacrifice for her sake, enables them to take an intelligent interest in her economic development and teaches them the important lesson of co-operating with one another for a national end...But the movement on its material side is an economic one, and through self-denying ordinances, extensively entered into, must serve valuable economic purpose, namely, to ensure a ready consumption of such articles as are production by keeping the demand for indigenous things largely in excess of the supply, the difficulties that surround the question economically are so great that they require the co-operation of every available agency to surmount them."[9]

Gokhale, thus, had a comprehensive conception of *Swadeshi*. Like Ranade, he felt that the key-problem in India was that of production which involved the utilization of capital and entrepreneurship. India was deficient in these fields and hence anyone who contributed to these aspects was working towards Swadeshism. So far as cotton fabrics were concerned, not even the most pronounced advocates of free trade could take objection to their increasing promotion in the country, because for the manufacture of cotton goods India had plenty of cheap labour and cotton. However, though Gokhale favoured *Swadeshi*, the more extreme technique of boycott did not receive his approval.

At the Banaras Congress, Gopal Krishna Gokhale categorised a set of nine demands for the realization of which immediate efforts had to be made: (i) a reform of the legislative councils by raising the proportion of elected members to one-half, and by requiring that the budgets be passed by the councils; (ii) the appointment of at least three Indians to the India Council; (iii) the creation of advisory boards in all districts throughout the country; the district magistrates were to consult these boards compulsorily in important matters of administration; (iv) the recruitment to the judicial branch of the Indian civil service from the ranks of the legal profession; (v) the separation of judicial and executive administration; (vi) the reduction of the heavy military expenditure; (vii) the expansion of primary education; (viii) the growth and extension of industrial and technical education, and (ix) the alleviation of rural indebtedness.[10] These demands represent in a summarized form the political philosophy of the Indian Moderates.

Gokhale was aware of the immense transformation that was being brought about in the Orient and he pleaded for a wise appreciation of the newer forces and ferment. He, hence, urged for the utilization of the surplus of the government revenue for implementing schemes of material and moral rehabilitation of the people. He even favoured government expenditure for enhancing production. In his budget speech of 1906, he said:

"...the improvement of the condition of the masses and the conciliation of the educated classes are the two really great problems before the British Government in India...There is but one way in which this conciliation can be secured, and that is by associating these classes more and more with government of their own country...the whole East is today throbbing with a new impulse—vibrating with a now passion—and it is not to be expected that India alone should continue unaffected by changes that are in the very air around us. We could not remain outside this influence even if we would. We would not so remain if we could...A volume of new feeling is gathering which requires to be treated with care. New generations are rising up, whose notions of the character and ideals of British rule are derived only from their experience of the last few years whose minds are not restrained by the thought of the great work which England has on the whole accomplished in the past in this land. I fully believe that it is in the power of the Government to give a turn to this feeling, which will make it a source of strength and not of weakness to the Empire."[11]

The emergence of new political and economic problems had divided the Congress into the Moderates and the new group of Extremist Nationalists. The seething discontent in the country made Gokhale alarmed and as the spokesman of the educated sections he supported "constitutional agitation" in his speeches at Allahabad. In the Imperial Legislative Council he made emphatic protest against the Seditious Meetings Bill.

Gokhale was perturbed by the rise of feelings of tension in the country and, hence, in 1906 he placed in the Imperial Legislative Council a Seven-point Scheme for the moral and material advancement of the Indian people: (i) the reduction of the state demand upon land, especially in U.P., Bombay and Madras (this would be a measure to provide some relief against the prevailing agricultural depression; (ii) to rescue the agriculturists from the load of crushing debts;) (iii) the establishment of Agricultural Banks like the one introduced in Egypt by Cromer, (iv) irrigation and scientific agriculture; (v) promotion of agricultural and technical education in the country; (vi) to make primary education free in all schools throughout the country; and (vii) to foster sanitary improvement.[12]

Decentralization is one of the primary themes of a philosophy of political rights. Centralization becomes tantamount to monocratic exercise of power. Gopal Krishna Gokhale recognized the necessity of decentralization. He wanted to provide checks on the actions of the bureaucracy on the spot. He advocated that provincial decentralization could succeed if the provincial councils were enlarged and were given the power of discussing the provincial budget. He had the keenness to recommend the formation of advisory district councils to advise the collector on questions of district administration. In his evidence before the Hobhouse Decentralization Commission, on March 7,1908, Gokhale recognized the necessity of, (i) village panchayats at the bottom, (ii) district councils at the intermediate level, and (iii) reformed legislative councils at the top.[13]

In a significant speech on "Students and Politics" on October 9, 1909, Gokhale analysed the genesis, achievements and failures of the new school of political thought. According to him three factors accounted for the emergence of the new school—(i) prevalence of a scene of "gloom" and frustration among the people during the latter part of Curzon's Viceroyalty, (ii) apparent failure of the Indian National Congress to achieve constitutional and administrative reforms, and (iii) absence of "political judgment" among a large number of people resulting in the acceptance of "ready-made opinions". He said: "The bulk of the remits of thc new school came from the ranks of our students, and though many of the elderly adherents of that school have, by now, been more or less disillusioned about the practicality of their programme, I fear its hold over its student followers is still as strong as before." Gokhale candidly acknowledged that the new school taught patriotism sacrifice and self exertion. But, unfortunately, it was directed to the destruction of the very foundations of the old public life of the country", and its chief weakness was that it ascribed all the troubles in the country "to the existence of a foreign government in the country," thereby ignoring the consideration of a problem in historical perspectives.[14]

In July 1911, the Universal Races Congress was held in London where Gokhale read a paper on "East and West in India", wherein he pleaded for the determination of Indo-British relations in the changed framework of the Euro-Asian political equations. The resurgence in Japan, China, India, Persia, Turkey and Egypt was the unequivocal manifestation of a new spirit in the old world. In this perspective it was essential that England should make a categorical declaration regarding her commitment to promote the growth of representative institutions in India and she should firmly adhere to that. Furthermore, the British administrative personnel in India had to be imbued with sentiments of conscientious and purposeful responsibility for the realisation of the good of the people. The British officials in India were to be representative of her best traditions and heritage. In the Indian world, their behaviour ought to be governed by canons of property and decency, otherwise, antipathetic reactions were bound to be general.

Gokhale was aware of the tremendous problems posed by the spread of English education in India. English education generated a greater responsiveness to the appreciation of liberty and the value of free institutions. He put forward certain criteria by which the ability of the Government to meet the new situation was to he judged. He said in 1911 :

"I suggest four tests to judge whether the Government is progressive, and further whether it is continuously progressive. The first test that I would apply is what measures it adopts for the moral and material improvement of the mass of people, and under these measures I do not include those appliances of modern governments which the British Government has applied in this country, because they were appliances necessary for its very existence, though they have benefited the people, such as the construction of Railways, the introduction of Posts and Telegraphs, and things of that kind. By measures for the moral and the material improvement of the people, I mean what the Government does for education, what the Government does for sanitation, what the Government does for agricultural development and so forth; That is my first test. The second test that I would apply is what steps the Government takes to give us a large share in the administration of our local affairs—in municipalities and local boards. My third test is what voice the Government gives us in its Councils—in those deliberative assemblies, where policies are considered. And, lastly, we must consider how far Indians are admitted into the ranks of the public service."[15]

Nation-Building and Community-Consciousness

Gokhale was highly sensitive to the problems of nation-building in a land of diversities. But he wanted the Hindu community to help others who were lower down in the scale in terms of command over economic goods and services. He urged upon the rulers of the state to realize the importance of the majority community. He said:

"It was urged that the Mohamedans badly ruled in India for

five centuries. It must not however be forgotten that the Hindus had ruled for countless centuries before them and even afterwards, before the British came on the scene, the Mohamedan power had been broken and displaced over nearly the whole country by a revival of Hindu rule. Then it was said that there were large Mohamedan populations in other countries—some of them self-governing countries—and that invested the Mohamedans of India with special importance. Mr. Gokhale could not see how that mattered in determining the extent of the representation which the Government of India should grant to its own subjects, unless it was on the assumption that in the administration of this country, those whose heart was not with India were to have preference over those whose was."[16]

He wanted the social and religious leaders in the country to realize the feelings of the Hindus:

"Not only was there no disposition among the Hindus to exalt or to feel triumphant but there was actually a sullen feeling of resentment throughout the country, a feeling daily growing deeper and stronger that the Government had not held the balance even and that it had already leaned too much on the Mohamedan side."[17]

Gokhale realized that the Hindu community although "mild and passive" temperamentally was plagued by the disfunctional element of castes. Hence the transformation of sub-systemic goals into aggregated demands of the community as a whole was made difficult. The positive task of nation-building required the cultivation of such maxims, norms, rules and values as were rooted in the desire for the furtherance of the material and moral good of all inhabitants. He wanted dedicated pursuit of social assimilationist, co-operative, educational and cultural activities for building the organic strength of a political system based on plurality patterns but owing allegiance to the nation. There was a sense of urgency, immediacy and keenness in Gokhale's writings and speeches but his spirit was entirely different from that of the disgrunted anarchists and revolutionists who were irrevocably alienated against the existing power-structure and condemned it in parochial system catering to the interests of the white elites.

To a limited extent only he was in favour of separate electorate for the Muslim community. In a note submitted to the Secretary of State, Gokhale had proposed:

"To throw open a substantial minimum of seats to election on a territorial basis, in which all qualified to vote should take part without distinction of race or creed. And then supplementary elections should be held for the minorities which, numerically or otherwise, are important enough to need special representation; these supplementary elections should be confined to the minorities only."[18]

Constitutional Testament

Towards the end of his life Gopal Krishna Gokhale formulated a plan for India–constitutional advance in consultation with Pherozeshah Mehta and the Aga Khan. His scheme was designed to lead to some form of federalism after some years. For the present (1914-15) he accepted the powers of intervention of the Governor-General. Gokhale's scheme recognized the limited need for separate and direct representation of Moslems and other minorities. He did not agree with the Aga Khan in advocating the ethnic reshapement of provinces.

The main items with the rather sensational proposal regarding Indian colonization of German Fast Africa, in Gokhale's Testament, regarding post-World War One reforms in India were:

(1) Acceptance of Provincial Autonomy.
(2) The English Governor to be helped by an Executive Council of six members of whom three shall be Indians.
(3) A Legislative Council consisting of 75 to 100 members of whom not less than 80 per cent should be elected.
(4) "The relations between the Executive Government and the Legislative Council so constituted should be roughly similar to those between the Imperial Government and the Reichstag in Germany. The Council will have to pass all Provincial legislation and its assent will be necessary in additions to or changes in Provincial taxation. The Budget too will have to come to it for discussion and its resolutions in connection with it, as also on questions of general

administration will have to be given effect to, unless vetoed by the Governor. More frequent meetings of longer continuous sittings will also have to be provided for. But the members of the Executive Government shall not depend, individually or collectively, on the support of a majority of the Council, for holding the offices."

(5) The provincial government to have complete charge of the internal administration of the province.

(6) Liberalizing of district administration and extension of local self-government.

(7) The Viceroyal Executive Council to consist of six members of whom two shall always be Indians.

(8) The Legislative Council to be designated as the Legislative Assembly of India.

(9) Commissions in the army and navy to be even to the inhabitants of the land.

(10) "German East Africa, if conquered from the Germans, should be reserved for Indian colonization and should be handed over to the Government of India."[19]

Gopal Krishna Gokhale was a historian and a professor of economics. Along with Dadabhai Naoroji and Ranade, he was in economic foundations of politics. The strength of the extremist leaders, like Tilak, Pal and Aurobindo, lay in a deep and profound study of India's vast philosophical and theological literature. Hence they quoted the *Bhagavad Gita* and the *Mahabharata*. But Dadabhai, Ranade and Gokhale were analytical student of science of political economy. The Extremists glorified the cultural attainments of ancient India. The Moderates spoke in the language of the classical economists and liberal politicians like Gladstone, Cobden and Mill. In generalized terms, with some degree of exaggeration, it can be said that the strength of the Moderates lay in economics, that of the Extremists in philosophy and religion.

Gokhale, although a keen economist, interested in problems of finance and income, had a moral approach to politics. Temperamentally, he was a spiritualist and a convinced idealist and lived on an elevated moral plane. His mission as a public leader has been "spiritualization of politics"—an ideal that was followed by Mahatma Gandhi. Gokhale would not sanction evil means to achieve a good end. He believed in the nobility of human nature. He had won the affection of the British statesmen and public figures. The latter recognized his qualities as an extraordinarily gifted leader of men. He was compared to Gladstone and Asquith. He won the confidence of Morley although the latter was doubtful of Gokhale's abilities in the art of political management. Through his noble life of self-abnegation, conscientiousness and purposefulness, Gokhale has encouraged the pursuit of the moral approach to political questions and public obligations. But Gokhale although an idealist, was not a Platonic or Utopian Idealist. He accepted the concepts of negotiations, moderation and compromise. Like Gandhi, he believed in scrupulous, justice and exacting rectitude even to the opponents. In his speeches and actions he would not advocate extreme measures. He would like to work out a synthesis between idealism and the realistic demands of the situation. Gokhale clung to the constitutional methods of agitation. He emphatically declared his faith in the unlimited potentialities of India. He would set no limits to the political aspirations of Indians. But as part of the processes of realistic adjustment to the needs of the times, he advocated the acceptance of Morley-Minto Reforms and worked on the Islington Commission for the Indianization of service. Gokhale's contribution to Indian political thought can be summed up in two basic propositions : (i) He stood for the introduction of moral values in politics; and (ii) he advocated moderation, reason and compromise as political techniques.

REFERENCES

1. *Speeches of Gopal Krishna Gokhale*, p. 1023.
2. *Ibid.*, p. 754
3. *Ibid.*
4. *Ibid.*, pp. 36-37.
5. *Ibid.*, pp. 900-901.
6. *Ibid.*, p. 88.
7. *Ibid.*
8. Nanda, B.R., *Gokhale, op. cit.*, pp. 169-72.

9. Zaidi, A.M. and Others, *The Encyclopaedia of Indian National Congress*, Vol. V, 1901-1905, op. cit., pp. 685-712.
10. *Ibid.*
11. *Speeches and Writings of Gopal Krishna Gokhale, op. cit.*, pp. 186-88.
12. *Ibid.*, p. 724.
13. *Ibid.*
14. *Ibid.*, p. 1006.
15. Quoted in Annie Besant's Presidential Address at the Calcutta Conference of 1917.
16. *Speeches of Gopal Krishna Gokhale*, p. 999.
17. *Ibid.*, p. 1000.
18. Deogirikar, T.R., *Gopal Krishna, op. cit.*, p. 94.
19. *Speeches of Gopal Krishna Gokhale*, pp. 10-25 to 29.

5

ECONOMIC AND FISCAL IDEAS

Among the Indian political leaders of the last generation few showed an understanding of the economic and fiscal problems then facing the country, and of the need for and the direction of reform in this field, more complete than Gopal Krishna Gokhale. His record in the Imperial Legislative Council, of which he was a member from 1902 until his death in 1915, shows that he was undoubtedly the greatest authority on public finance of his time in India.

Poverty in India

At the time when Gokhale entered the Supreme Legislative Council, and for several decades previously, the dominant economic problem, which engrossed the attention of statesmen and publicists, was and had been the problem of poverty of the masses. That India was, on the whole, a very poor country, that the mass of the people enjoyed only a scanty subsistence, and were, therefore, impatient of taxation, had been recognized by Anglo-Indian statesmen very soon after the transfer of India from the Company to the Grown. Since the establishment of the East India Association in 1867, Dadabhai Naoroji[1] had brought this question prominently before that body and before the public. The frequency of famines in the second half of the 19th century (there was a famine in Orissa in 1866, one in 1873-74 in Bihar, in 1876-78 in Madras and Bombay, in 1896 over the whole of the country with the exception of Bengal, and the worst one in 200 years, affecting nearly half the country, in 1900) and the loss of life occasioned by them (the Orissa famine alone carried off a million and a half), emphasised the seriousness of the problem. With the establishment of the National Congress in 1885, the subject of Indian poverty became a constant theme of speeches at the national gathering. The second Congress, at Calcutta, held under the presidency of Dadabhai Naoroji, gave a prominent place to a resolution on poverty. It resolved that "this Congress regards with the deepest sympathy, and views with grave apprehension, the increasing poverty of vast numbers of the population of India, etc."[2]

Whether the poverty of India was in fact increasing or decreasing soon became a matter of controversy. The official view was that though the poverty was undoubted, it was gradually diminishing. The exponents of this view pointed to such things as the Import of precious metals into the country, the increasing revenue under customs and excise, and stamps, etc. in support of their view. In his Budget speech of 1901, Lord Curzon said that the national Income of India, which had been calculated at Rs. 27 per head in 1882, had now risen to Rs. 30. This argument, however, ignored the fact that the level of prices in 1900 was at least 26 per cent higher than in 1882.[3] Gokhale had been already cross-examined on the subject of the condition of the agricultural classes when he appeared before the Welby Commission in 1897. The question was, as he said, somewhat outside that Commission's terms of reference and therefore, he had not gone into it in detail, but in his Budget speech of 1902 he devoted considerable attention to the subject, and made out a convincing case in support of his view about 'deep and deepening poverty'.[4] It is noteworthy that in his concluding remarks, Lord Curzon made no attempt to reply to Gokhale's argument, but contented himself with saying that he agreed with his Finance Member in regarding the increased receipts from customs, stamps, excise, Post office evidence of increasing prosperity. The Finance Member had observed that it was wrong to suppose that the increase in the returns from Customs etc. indicated only "the prosperity of a small class, whilst the majority of the people are in distress. There might be grounds for such an idea, if we found our Customs returns increasing, only or out of proportion, from importation of articles of luxury; if we found our railway receipts increasing, out of proportion, from first and second class traffic; if we found out Postal Savings,

Bank deposits increasing chiefly in the accounts of the large depositors or, if we found our income-tax returns from the large incomes, rapidly augmenting; but it is the opposite of all this that is the case. As I have pointed out, it is from import duties on articles consumed by the agricultural and poorer classes, that we obtain rapidly increasing returns; it is from goods and third class passenger traffic that our railways have prospered; it is the small investors who multiply and increase their deposits in the Postal Savings Banks; and our income-tax returns from incomes above Rs. 2,000 per annum, which fail to meet our reasonable anticipations".[5] Returning to the subject in his Budget speech of 1903, Gokhale said in reply that if the imports showed an increase in cotton goods used by the poorer classes, this was only evidence of the ruin of the indigenous cotton industry; that a few paltry increase in revenue under certain heads did not deserve to be taken seriously as conclusive evidence of growing prosperity; and that such incontrovertible facts as an increasing death-rate, independently of famine and plague, and increasing rural indebtedness, showed that the poverty of the country was not only deep, but deepening.

What were the causes of this 'deep and deepening' poverty of the country, and what were to be the remedies ? Dadabhai Naoroji traced it to the annual drain of wealth from the country, caused by the use of foreign agency for the administration of the country. He accordingly laid very great stress on the substitution of native for foreign agency as far as possible, and with a view to this, on Simultaneous Examinations for recruitment to the Imperial Services. In moving the resolution for Simultaneous Examinations at the first Congress, he used these words: "The resolution which I propose to you is of the utmost possible importance to India. It is the most important key to our material and moral advancement. All our other political reforms will benefit us but very little indeed if this reform of all reforms is not made. It is the question of life and death to India. It is the question of questions,[6] D.E. Wacha moved the resolution on Poverty in the second Congress, and he too said that 'one of the very first and most important remedies', though according to him not the only one, was 'to minimize the foreign agency.'[7] But as there seemed no prospect of any reform being carried out until the Indian leaders succeeded in attaining a position whence their protests and appeals could be respectfully heared. The resolution demanded introduction of representative institutions as one of the most important practical steps towards the amelioration of the condition of the people.

It is refreshing to find that the discussion on this resolution revealed a consciousness on the part of the delegates of the great complexity of the problem. A member from Madras (Rao Bahadur A. Sabapathy Mudaliar) said that he was certainly in favour of the resolution, but realised that even after establishing representative government, people will have to understand that the chief causes which have brought about the great poverty of India are not all political.[8] Another, Pandit Jwalauth Sarma, from Calcutta, raised the question of population: "We should see whether it is any undue increase in the population which prevents them being supplied with food, or the scantiness of the production due to imperfect agriculture, or the neglect of industrial arts that makes us poor. We must look into all causes; we must realise... it is not because of a single cause but of a great many causes."[9] Another member referred to the ruin of Indian industries: " Ono cause of this increasing poverty is the manner in which the production of most of the manufactured necessaries of life, clothing, tools, implements, etc., has been diverted from the hands of our countrymen into those of foreign manufacturers. I do think that with a considerable body of our people in the several councils, means would be found to revive our ancient industries and establish new industries, so that as time went on all our requirements in this line should be supplied to us by our own artisans."[10] And yet another said that if the indigenous industries were ruined, "this is not so much the fault of England as our own fault. We should try to compete with England by establishing such institutions as would support our own artisans, and by purchasing things from them." This last is an echo of the *Swadeshi* movement, which had been started in Poona by Ganesh Vasudoo Joshi, better known as Sarvajanik Kaka, as early as 1869. The question of population too was broached as early as 1878 in an article in the second number of the Quarterly of the Poona Sarvajanik Sabha, entitled 'Overpopulation and Marriage Customs.' The article is unsigned, but it is not unlikely that it was from the pan of M.G. Ranade. Ranade's concern with the problem of population is evidenced by his paper on Indian Emigration, written in 1893, in which he speaks of emigration as affording a solution, even if partial, to the economic problems of India. The favourite idea of Ranade and Rao Bahadur G.V. Joshi was that in the then existing conditions of India, when old Indian industries had been ruined by the competition of English machine-made goods, by the policy of Free Trade, and by the extension of Railways, it was the duty of the State to foster new industries—firstly, by giving protection to infant industries, but if political considerations did not allow this, then by subsidizing, and in other ways supporting new industries. "In truth, there is no difference of principle," wrote Ranade, "between lending such support and guidance, by the free use of its Credit and superior organisation, in pioneering Industrial undertakings, or subsidizing private co-operative effort, and its guaranteeing minimum interest to Railway Companies."[11] State action in various forms, for 'Simultaneous Examinations', for promoting technical education, for reducing the burden of taxation, particularly by the introduction of a permanent settlement, and for economy in administration, and in particular reduction in military expenditure, was also called for by the Indian National Congress, and year after year resolutions were passed in this sense at its sessions. Excessive military expenditure was criticised even by a non-official European member—Sir Griffith Evans at the budget session of the Imperial Legislative Council in 1893. He also criticised the Home Charges, and "the tendency on the part of the various departments in England to shove everything they can on India; e.g. mission to Persia or China." The India Office charges also appeared to be on a lavish scale. Indeed, this particular abuse—charging India with expenses which did not legitimately belong to her—had been drawn attention to by Henry Fawcett in the House of Commons as early as 1870.

Most of these arguments and suggestions we find adopted and developed by Gokhale. Contrary to Ranade, he made efforts, to stop Indian emigration. In 1910, he moved in the Imperial Legislative Council that the Government should be empowered to prohibit the recruitment of indentured labour for the colony of Natal. When the

Government actually stopped such recruitment, he congratulated them. In 1912, again, he moved a resolution recommending the prohibition of recruitment of indentured labour altogether, and made one of his finest speeches—perhaps the finest speech in moving it. As the resolution was opposed by the Government, rejection was inevitable, but it is noteworthy that the biggest vote that Gokhale ever obtained on any of his resolutions which were opposed by Government was obtained on this. The reason why Gokhale opposed the system of indentured labour, and put such noble passion and eloquence into his speech against it, was that the system had led to great abuses, and he felt it was an insult to India's national honour. Even Ranade had observed in his article which wrote in 1893:

"Without a strict enforcement of the Protection Laws in their interest by the Government of India, the Coolie Emigrants would not be able to hold their own against the greed of their Employers, the Planters, who are not generally noted for their humanity. The Magistracy and the Government machinery in these Colonies, being entirely in the hands of the white population, are not very impartial in their treatment of the Indian settlers." "But notwithstanding these disadvantages, "Ranade went on to say, "there can be no doubt that the system of Protected Emigration has, on the whole, been very beneficial." The condition envisaged by Ranade - strict enforcement of the Protection Laws—had, however, not been fulfilled, and the system had bred 'frightful immorality' and led to 'appalling human misery.'[12] Gokhale's whole soul revolted against it. "There are disabilities enough in all conscience", he said in his 1912 speech, "attaching to our position in this country.... Why must this additional brand be put upon our brow before the rest of the civilised world ?" "India is the only country which supplies indentured labour at the present moment. Why should India be marked out for this degradation?"[13] It is perhaps the most powerful of Gokhale's speeches in this volume, and it is impossible to read it, even at this distant date, without being moved.

Gokhale did not lay much stress on the drain of wealth from India to England, of which Dadabhai Naoroji made so much. It is true that in his evidence before the Welby Commission, he conceded to Dadabhai that Indians were not able themselves to develop new industries because the capital was carried away from the country. If the capital had remained in the country, we might have been much better able to take advantage of those resources. In his 1907 speech on the Swadeshi Movement, Gokhale puts: "the annual cost to India of England's political domination... at 20 crores of rupees... it is incumbent that our men should be employed more and more in the service of the State, so that Pensions and furlough charges might be saved to the country." These are, however, about the only references in Gokhale's speeches to the subject of the drain, and on the whole he kept it out of sight. No doubt he felt, as did Ranade, that to hold "that as long as we have a heavy tribute to pay to England,... we are doomed and can do nothing to help ourselves" was 'hardly a fair or manly position to take up.'[14]

Gokhale felt the humiliation involved in alien rule, but he considered that in the peculiar circumstances of the country, progress was possible only through the continuance of British rule. Instead of inveighing, therefore, against the drain of wealth from the country, he devoted himself to a study of the country's finances, (and with what thoroughness did he study them!) and showed to the officials, with convincing arguments, and facts and figures to support them, how they could be administered for the greater good of the people. For some years before 1902, when Gokhale made his debut in the Imperial Legislative Council, Indian finances had shown large surpluses. Indian Finance Ministers and Secretaries of State for India had looked upon these surpluses as irrefutable evidence of India's prosperity, and at the Budget Session of 1902, Speaker after Speaker had congratulated the Finance Member on the surplus shown by the revised estimates of 1901-02. The very first sentence of Gokhale's speech struck a note of dissent. "Your Excellency, I fear I cannot conscientiously join in the congratulations which have been offered to the Hon'ble Finance Member on the huge surplus which the revised estimates show for last year." He pointed out that "the surpluses were merely currency surpluses, due to the artificial raising of the value of the rupee, and the result, therefore, of veiled additional taxation." Gokhale argued that a system under which surpluses accrued for years in succession, was an unsound system, because a surplus meant "so much more money taken from system, because a surplus meant "so much more money taken from the people, either through miscalculation or in other ways, than was needed for the requirements of Government."[15] They were, moreover, dangerous, because they constituted 'a direct invitation to the Government to increase expenditure,' and 'a temptation to the authorities in England to shift a portion of their own burden to the shoulders of the Indian Government.' Large surpluses were, therefore, wrong in themselves, but if they did occur, they should be utilized either for the remission of taxation, e.g. for reducing the duties on salt, raising the minimum limits for liability to income-tax, reducing the burden on the land. In the temporarily-settled Provinces, taking of the excise duties on cotton, etc. ; or for promoting nation building activities such as education, sanitation and medical relief, Gokhale repeated these demands year after year in the Imperial Council.

Schemes for Improvement

In his 1906 speech, he gave his view of what a 'comprehensive scheme' for improving the condition of the masses might be. This would include: (i) reduction in the State demand on land, (ii) composition of rural debts, (iii) cheap credit to the agriculturists in case of genuine need, (iv) Irrigation and Scientific Agriculture, (v) Industrial and Technical Education, (vi) Free, and later, Compulsory Primary Education, and (vii) Works of Sanitary Improvement.[16] Surpluses should be utilised for such objects as these, and not for reduction of the unproductive debt of the country, which was so small that its further reduction was not a matter of much importance, nor for building of railways, which should be conducted out of borrowings, and not from surpluses, which, being 'so much more revenue taken from the people than was necessary for the requirements of Government,' should be spent on works needed urgently for their welfare. Gokhale's contention in his Budget speeches that surpluses should not be utilized for the construction of Railways, may at first sight, be seen to run directly counter to the view maintained by him before the Welby Commission, that railroads should be built out of surpluses, and not out of borrowed capital.

that both the surpluses and railways were different in 1897 from what they became in 1902 and the following years. In 1897 the era of large surpluses had not yet begun; and the Railways were still a losing concern. In 1898-99, began the era of large surpluses, and Railways also began to yield a surplus from the turn of the century.

Besides surpluses and their proper use, the other point which Gokhale emphasized in his Budget Speeches was the need of reduction. In the military budget and of Indianization of the Services, he had already emphasized that in his evidence before the Welby Commission.

Till 1909, the only opportunity which non-official members of the Legislative Council had of criticizing the administration and making suggestions was at the time of the annual budget, and even then it was not open to them to move resolutions and divide the Council on them. Under the Morley-Minto Reforms, they obtained this right, under certain conditions, and Gokhale used it to press his favourite idea that surpluses should be used for promoting the welfare of the people. Such were his resolutions on Surpluses and Sanitation in 1910, on Surpluses and Provincial Reserves in 1912, and on the Opium Fund in 1911. He also moved resolutions for effecting reduction in the expenditure of various departments, e.g., Telegraphs, Stationery and Printing, Railways, Mint, Salt, Police, etc. with the double object of effecting economies, and of drawing attention to the paucity of Indian personnel in the various departments. His anxiety to see that all available resources should be utilised for ameliorative measures, instead of for reduction of unproductive debt, led him also to propose in 1913 that the cost of building New Delhi should be met not from current revenue, but from loans, and that a Committee be appointed to inquire into the adequacy or otherwise of the resources of Local Bodies, which were the authorities directly concerned with people's education, sanitation, and medical relief. All these proposals were either withdrawn or rejected by large majorities. However, it may be admitted that in very few cases, they served their purpose. Thus Gokhale's criticism of the working expenses of Railways in 1910 brought about some improvement next year.[17]

Reduction in Salt Duties

To his plea in his very first speech in the Imperial Legislative Council, that with large continuous surpluses for four years, it was wrong to maintain taxation at the existing level, the reply on the official side was, firstly, that they could not be absolutely sure about future surpluses, and secondly, that they could not reduce revenue at a time when they had increased expenditure in view and that in directions which Gokhale would approve, such as education, police, public works, and sanitation. Yet next year, the Government did carry out two of Gokhale's suggestions, viz., reduction of the salt duty, and the raising of the taxable minimum for income-tax from Rs. 500 to Rs. 1,000. In 1904 Gokhale urged further reduction in the salt duty, and this too was conceded in 1905. Small grants were also made in the same year for education, for Police reform, and in aid of Local Boards, Gokhale's suggestions for relieving Local Boards from responsibility for famine relief for still further reduction of the salt duty, for grants to Local Boards for sanitation, were also acted upon in course of time. His plea that surpluses should not be used for reduction of debt, however, met with a different treatment at the hands of Government. "I am afraid" said Sir James Meston, the Finance Secretary, in 1911, "that in this respect, between the conservatism of the Finance Department and the radical optimism of the Hon'ble Member (meaning Gokhale), there is a great gulf fixed over which I cannot pretend to throw a bridge. Gokhale honestly believes that we make a fetish of this reduction of our unproductive debt...We on our side believe equally honestly that the presence of our unproductive debt is an incubus and that its growth is a danger to be averted to the beat of our ability...

Reduction in Army Expenditure

Gokhale's pleas for reduction in army expenditure, and in the demand from land, and for abolition of the excise on cotton, did not fare any better at the hands of Government. In vain, Gokhale urged again and again that the strength of the army (230,000 men) was far in excess of what the 1879 Army Commission itself had considered to be sufficient for India's needs (i.e. 180,000 men); that General Brackenbury, who was Military Member of the Imperial Council at one time, had himself admitted in his evidence before the Welby Commission that the Indian army was in excess of India's own requirements that the defeat of Russia at the hands of Japan (1905) and later the conclusion of the Anglo-Russian Convention (1907) had removed the threat from Russia, rendering possible a reduction in the strength of the army; and that the fact that a considerable portion of the Indian Army could be spared for service in South Africa and China, showed that its strength was in excess of Indian requirements. Alluding to this last argument, which had been made more than once from the platform of the Indian National Congress, Lord Curzon said in his Budget Speech of 1900: "Let not any one carry away the idea that because for a few months or even for a year, we have been able to spare 8,000 of our British troops for Africa, the British garrison in India can be permanently reduced by that amount. There can be no more complete or foolish illusion. Because a man lends for a night the watchdog that guards his home to a neighbour who is being attacked by robbers, does it therefore follow that his own house will be able to get on in future without protection?"[19] The imperious Proconsul was not very happy with his argument, because, as events turned out, the Indian troops remained in South Africa not 'for a few months or even for a year', but for three years.

Textile Excise

The case of the excise duties on cotton was as bad, or perhaps worse. When in 1894 financial exigencies led to the imposition of import duties after an interval of 12 years (since 1882 India had boon almost entirely free), cotton manufactures were excluded from the schedule. The omission was criticized not only by Indian members of the Council, like Gangadharrao Chitnavis, Fazulbhoy Vishram, Rash Behari Ghose and the Maharaja of Darbhanga, but also by representatives of the European trading community like Playfair and Sir Griffith Evans (both from Calcutta), and even a Bengal

Civilian, Charles Stevens (later Sir Stevens, and Lieutenant Governor of Bengal). A few days later, in the course of his speech on the Financial Statement for 1894-95, Sir Griffith Evans referred to the matter again, and spoke of the pressure brought by a Lancashire deputation on the Secretary of State. "After a few stock phrases about disinterested concern for the poor Indian, they showed their tooth, and gave him to understand very plainly that they would do their best to turn out any Ministry that opposed what they considered the interest of the trade, and pointed out that Lancashire was strong enough to win any fight she went into in earnest."[20] Later in the year, cotton goods were included in the schedule, but a countervailing excise duty was imposed on Indians which was supposed to enter into competition with Lancashire. Still later, in 1896, the import duty was lowered from 5 per cent to 3½ per cent, and same amount of excise duty was imposed on all Indian cotton manufactures, coarse or fine, whether entering into competition with Lancashire or not. And there the duty remained till 1926, a constant reminder to India of the essential character of colonialism. "The excise duties have done" an English writer has said, "more than any other administrative act of the British in India in modern times, to impair the moral basis upon which the British control is supposed to rest."[21]

Gokhale spoke of the cotton duties in 1902, 1903 and 1904. After 1904, he made no mention of the subject for several years' more, perhaps because after 1904 the worst days of the cotton mill industry seemed to be over, and soon 'a great wave of prosperity passed over the industry'. When Gokhale returned to the subject in 1911, it was to support a resolution moved by the Hon'ble Dadabhoy for abolition of the excise duties. But he made it clear that he supported the resolution not in the interests of the manufacturers, but in that of the consumers, on whom the duty ultimately fell, and who were the poorest of the poor. And suggested that the duty might be abolished only in the case of counts below 30, and retained for those above. This was characteristic of Gokhale. He considered Indian economic problems from the standpoint of the toiling millions, and not from that of the rich few, even though the Servants of India Society, which he bad founded in 1905, found some of its chief supporters among the millionaire manufacturers. Thus, in 1911, when a bill to amend the law relating to Labour in Indian Factories came up for consideration, Gokhale moved an amendment imposing on the factory-owners the duty of giving free and compulsory education to children employed in the factories. When Pandit Madan Mohan Malaviya moved a Resolution proposing protection for the Indian sugar industry, Gokhale observed that the first question to be considered in connection with the resolution was how a measure of protection would affect the cultivator. In 1912 he would not even support Dadabhoy's proposal to raise the minimum limit for income-tax from Rs. 1,000 to Rs. 1,500, because such a measure would give relief to the middle class, whereas it was the poorer classes of the country who deserved relief earlier than the upper or the middle classes, since they bore a heavier burden, relatively to their resources, than the latter.

Police Debt

It was in keeping with Gokhale's concern for the welfare of the poor agriculturist that when in 1904 Government brought in a bill for the constitution and control of Co-operative Credit Societies, Gokhale welcomed it cordially as a measure bearing promise of bringing some relief to the agriculturist and of evoking and strengthening in him "those qualities of prudence, thrift, self-reliance and resourcefulness, without which outside help can do him no great or permanent good." He suggested several improvements in the measure, such as modification of the principle of unlimited liability, Nation of the separate societies to a Central Bank, etc., which were carried out subsequently.

Gold Exchange Standard

Prices had begun to rise in India from about 1905, and the matter had begun to cause anxiety by 1908. Gokhale referred to it in his Budget Speeches of 1908 and 1909. He thought that the rise of prices had something to do with the heavy additions to the currency made by Government. The question of currency had assumed unusual importance at this time. The position, briefly, was this. Since 1835 there had been one standard rupee in British India, and the mints had been opened to the coinage of silver on private account. The gold value of the rupee depended on the gold price of silver bullion, and it was round about 1/10th of the sovereign for about 40 years. From 1873 onwards, however, silver, and therefore, the rupee began to decline rapidly in value, in terms of gold. This caused great embarrassment to the Government of India in meeting its sterling obligations in England, and also upset the country's trade with gold using countries.

On the recommendation of the Herschell. Committee, therefore, it was decided in 1893 to give up the silver standard in favour of a gold standard, and, as a first step, the mints were closed to the free coinage of silver, the object being to divorce the value of the rupee from that of silver bullion, and to raise, or rather to arrest the fail of its value through limitation of the number of rupees in circulation. At the same time it was declared that gold coin and bullion would be received at the mints in exchange for rupees at the rate of 1s. 4d. to the rupee, and that sovereigns and half-sovereigns would be similarly received at Government treasuries in payment of sums due to Government. This policy was successful, and by 1899 the value of the rupee rose to 1s. 4d. The rupee thus became a token coin, with the artificial value of 16d., whereas its intrinsic value was only 10d. The problem was how to keep it steady at that rate. The readiness with which Government supplied rupees in exchange for gold or sovereigns, and the declaration, in 1899, of the sovereign as legal tender (as recommended by the Fowler Committee of 1898) prevented the value of the rupee from rising above 1s. 4d., while Government's readiness—(not as unqualified as in the former me, and not legally binding)—to supply sovereigns at the rate of 1s. 4d. a rupee, and to sell sterling bills payable in London at about the same rate, prevented it from falling below 1s. 4d. Thus all difficulties which Government had experienced on account of the fall in exchange were set at rest. The exchange was kept steady, the budgets yielded large surpluses, and trade went on undisturbed. There was a crisis in 1907-08, when owing to a falling-off of Indian exports, the exchange became weak; but, by utilizing all the gold in its reserves, the Paper Currency Reserve and the Gold Standard Reserve (which had been created in 1900 from the profits of the rupee coinage, and kept in London, partly in the form of gold and partly in securities), and by raising a loan in England, Government was able to overcome the crisis and to maintain the exchange value of the rupee.

The system outlined above, which, being neither a purely silver standard nor a purely gold standard, came to be known as a Gold Exchange Standard. This worked satisfactorily till the First World War. Still, it gave rise to more than one question. In the first place, though it provided a solution to the exchange problem, and the allied problem of balancing the budget, it did so only by imposing additional taxation (in a valid manner). On the contrary, Gokhale made this point more than once, and on that ground argued for remission of taxation, etc. The currency had now become an artificial one; it was no longer automatic, as it had been before 1893, when the mints were open; rupees could now be coined only by the Government. The question was should the Government make additions to the currency at its own sweet will? Gokhale thought that this had happened, and that the marked rise of prices from about 1905 onwards was due to "phenomenally heavy coinage" by Government. He asked for "a close and immediate investigation by a competent body of men" into the question.[22] In replying to Gokhale, the Finance Member, Sir E. Biker, pointed out that the figures of coinage given by Gokhale for 1905-07 were not those of net coinage; Gokhale himself had said that he had not been able to get the figures of rupees recoined during that period and that if the figures of net coinage were taken, the coinage within 15 years since 1893 would be found to be about 51 crores a year, whereas in the 15 years, preceding the closing of the mints, it was about 7 crores a year. Further, that the rise of prices could not be due to redundancy of currency because it began in 1905, before there was a possibility of such redundancy; that the prices of other staples had not risen, like those of foodgrains; that the gold value of the rupee had not depressed in anything like the same proportion as the rise in the price of food grains; that prices had risen in other countries also besides India, e.g. in England, Germany, Egypt, and Japan; and finally that the additions to coinage made by Government had been only to meet the demands of trade, and "as long as Government refrained from coining rupees except upon demand of trade, there could be no dilution of the currency."[23]

Gokhale also supported the resolution of Sir Vithaldas, moved on the same day as that on the Gold Standard Reserve, for opinion of the mints to the free coinage of gold. Coining of gold in India had been contemplated ever since the closing of the mints to silver in 1893, and the Fowler Committee had recommended it. The recommendation was accepted both by the Government of India and the Secretary of State, and in 1900 the Finance Member, Sir Clinton Dawkins, announced in the Imperial Council that steps were being taken to constitute a branch of the Mint at Bombay for the coinage of gold. But the Royal Mint raised a number of difficulties, and the British Treasury also opposed the idea, and the plan was indefinitely postponed. The opposition of the Treasury was based on the ground that "gold currency was not necessary for the maintenance of the gold standard, that even without a gold currency India was able to obtain whatever gold she required, and that a gold currency would be expensive." These arguments were plausible enough, but public sentiment in India was in favour of a gold currency, and Government had to take up the matter again when Sir V. Thackersey moved resolutions on it in 1911 and 1912.

In 1912 Sir Guy Fleetwood Wilson gave a very sympathetic reply, and Sir Vithaldas withdrew his resolution. The matter was taken up by the Government of India with the Home authorities, but once more the British Treasury raised difficulties, and ultimately the question was referred, among others, to the Chamberlain Commission of 1913, which recommended that if Indian sentiment demanded a gold currency, and the Government of India were prepared to incur the expense, gold coins should be minted in India, but that it was not to India's advantage to use gold for internal circulation. The matter rested there, when the First World War broke out, creating new problems for Indian currency. As stated above, the arguments of the British Treasury and the Chamberlain Commission appeared plausible, but as remarked by Professor Cannan in his Foreword to Dr. Ambedkar's book on the "Problem of the Rupee", the expense involved in a gold currency would have been trifling, and as for India not needing a gold currency,[24] the position has been maintained not because India dislikes gold, but because Europeans like it so well that they cannot bear to part with any of it.

In view of the position taken by Gokhale in 1912, it may seem strange that speaking in 1907 he had argued against the adoption of gold currency. The question at that time, however, was about the purpose of and the limits to be put on the Gold Standard Reserve; Gokhale argued that it was not right to allow the Reserve to accumulate without limit, because it would never suffice to ensure the conversion of rupees into gold; and he hoped that if a limit were to be set to the Gold Standard Reserve, any further increase in it could be diverted, directly or indirectly, to nation-building activities. Moreover, Sir Vithaldas' resolution, which Gokhale supported, did not propose to substitute gold currency for silver, but merely to add a branch at the Mint for free coinage of gold.

In 1912, Gokhale again returned to the question of the use of the budget surpluses and moved a resolution recommending the creation of special provincial reserves by means of grants from the imperial surpluses. He said, "Money is required for non-recurring expenditure in many directions in this country, specially for education, sanitation and medical relief... These will require not ten but hundreds of crores of rupees and the problem cannot be satisfactorily dealt with unless the Government made large regular allotments for this purpose. The Government, however, is reluctant to make a large regular allotment out of the current revenues. Therefore, I propose another method which, though not equally satisfactory, will be found to answer the requirements to some extent... What I urge is that two-thirds of this surplus, as also all future surpluses, should be placed at the disposal of provincial governments for non-recurring expenditure on the objects I have mentioned. The present policy of making grants for a year only out of the surplus that accrues during that year is wasteful policy. The local governments cannot rely upon a continuance of their good fortune and, therefore, they cannot take in hand any large scheme which requires finances over a series of years ... The Government of India, on the other hand, can think only of a single surplus at a time, and therefore, it is not surprising that it does not find itself to make any further grant until another surplus is realized."[25]

These are a few illustrations of the depth of analysis and the breadth of vision that Gokhale brought to bear on the debates on the public finances of the country. Because of his ill-health, Gokhale did not attend the Council during the debate on the budget in 1913. Without him the debate must have been a tame affair. While most of the Council members were making speeches showering superlative praise and congratulations on the Finance Member, the Hon'ble Sir Guy Fleetweed Wilson must have sat there missing only one man, Gokhale. Winding up the debate, Sir Guy expressed himself in so many words: "I do not propose to detain the Council long to offer many remarks; but I should like to preface my remarks by saying how deeply I regret the absence of one who has proved himself to be a true servant of India and that is Mr. Gokhale...It is difficult for those who served in previous Councils to express to those who are new to this Council what a great blank Mr. Gokhale's absence creates. It seems to be a play of Hamlet without Hamlet."[26]

REFERENCES

1. Naoroji, Dadabhai, *Poverty and Un-British Rule in India* (New Delhi: Publications Division, Government of India), 1962.
2. *Ibid.*
3. *Speeches and Writings of Gopal Krishna Gokhale*, Vol. I, Economic (Bombay: Asia Publishing House), 1962, p. Introduction, xvi.
4. *Ibid.*, pp. 11-14.
5. *Ibid.*
6. Naoroji, Dadabhai, *Poverty and Un-British Rule in India, op. cit.*, p. 61.
7. Zaidi, A.M. and Others, *The Encyclopaedia of Indian National Congress*, Vol. I.
8. *Speeches and Writings of Gopal Krishna Gokhale*, Vol. I, op. cit., p. Introduction, xviii.
9. *Ibid.*
10. *Ibid.*
11. *Ibid.*
12. *Ibid.*, Introduction, xx.
13. *Ibid.*
14. *Ibid..*, p. 569.
15. *Ibid.*, p. 112.
16. *Ibid.*, p. 102-106.

17. *Ibid.*, pp. 369-84.
18. *Ibid.*, Introduction, xxiv.
19. *Ibid.*, p. 135.
20. *Ibid.*, pp. 7, 13
21. *Ibid.*
22. *Ibid.*, pp. 127-43.
23. *Ibid.*
24. Ambedkar, B.D., *Problem of Rupee* (Bombay: Thacker), 1939, Foreword.
25. Dandekar, V. M., "Economic and Fiscal Thinking of Gopal Krishna Gokhale", in Verinder Grover (ed.) *Gopal Krishna Gokhale* (New Delhi: Deep and Deep), 1991, pp. 131-132.
26. *Ibid.*

6

TILAK AND GOKHALE

Any attempt to label in general terms the philosophies of men so intimately and so long associated as were Tilak and Gokhale with the struggles and aspirations of their people is bound to prove inadequate. The same may be said to an even greater degree of the attempt to estimate their influence, individually or comparatively, on the course of Indian history. By what criteria can we satisfactorily judge how much the individual was a product of his times, and how much later times were fashioned by the ideas and actions of any great man? At best, therefore, these summary conclusions may serve as tentative appraisals of the philosophies of Tilak and Gokhale, while the influence of each upon India today can only be conjectured.

The social and political philosophies of Tilak and Gokhale developed initially from their different responses to the spread of Western ideology over the subcontinent of India in the wake of the consolidation of British rule. Gokhale was attracted by the humanitarianism and liberalism of progressive Western thought, which he avidly absorbed through the writings of men like Edmund Burke and John Stuart Mill, and the teachings of his great *guru* Ranade. He joined at an early age the mainstream reform of India's nationalist movement which had already received so powerful an impetus from the labours of pioneers like Ram Mohun Roy and Ranade. He was by no means blind to the misfortunes connected with India's subordinate political status, but he placed the blame for these more on the inequities and inadequacies of Hindu society, than the harsh exactions of a foreign imperialism. The introduction of British rule, in fact, was considered by Gokhale and his *guru* as the fortuitous dispensation of divine providence sent to rouse India from the lethargy of centuries and to teach her how to remodel her institutions in the image of the then most highly advanced nation of the world.

Tilak was initially steeped more in the lore of Hinduism than in the Western learning, and though introduced to the latter at almost as early an age as Gokhale, its poetry and philosophy struck no responsive chord in his mental make up. Under Professor Kerunna Chhatre's strong influence, Tilak delved more deeply into the study of mathematics and astronomy than into the humanities or social sciences, and later used this knowledge to bolster ideas he had already accepted on faith. With scant introduction to the highest ideals of Western thought and with an orthodox appreciation of the rich and profound heritage of his own people's culture, Tilak began to view British rule as a predatory foreign incubus rather than a blessing. Foreigners of the Christian faith had usurped the pre-minent hereditary status of his caste, and threatened to refashion India so that in time even the traditionally exalted position of Brahmans might be thoroughly undermined. These understandably grave apprehensions which Tilak shared with many descendants of the Peshwa's community were given powerful literary expression in the vitriolic Marathi essays of Vishnu Krishna Chiplunkar. Under Chiplunkar's influence, Tilak was soon drawn into the militant revivalist or revolutionary mainstream of India's nationalist movement. To Chiplunkar, Tilak and their followers, it was not the status of widows nor the age of marriage; not the ignorance of mothers, nor the disabilities of caste; not the inadequate development of a spirit of public service, nor unhygienic practices or superstition, which lay at the root of India's misery, poverty, and humiliation; but rather her loss of freedom alone, her subjugation to foreign rule. Indeed, from their orthodox viewpoint social conditions like those noted above, which to Western eyes were shocking debilities, did not demand public attention, certainly not legislative remedy. The utilitarian ethic had no exalted status in the traditional Hindu system of values. Individuals were what they deserved to be, thanks to their actions to countless prior existences, by the inexorable law of *Karma*. Each individual was to seek his own salvation along whatever path to *moksha* he was qualified to take by virtue of his social status and personal capacity. The universe was no laboratory for the experiments of social scientists, but rather a divinely ordered and totally integrated reflection of Brahma, sustained according to *dharma*. Indian history had not commenced with the advent of the British, and Hindu society regulated by its *shastras* in keeping with Vedic revelation was eternal, and needed no Christian or atheistic dogmas to teach it how to function. The foreigners were trying to subvert Hindu *dharma* by tampering with every sacred institution in the motherland, for the unscrupulous selfish purpose of strengthening their grasp over India, and bleeding her of her wealth more effectively. To aid and abet them in this utter spoliation of the colony which had been conquered by a combination of force and fraud, Englishmen enlisted the talents and services of countless Indians. Many Indians were Brahmans; who had sold their birth-right for an English suit of clothes, and ignored their own heritage and language, content to imitate the vulgar rulers in every degrading manner. How could such men but be characterized from Tilak's viewpoint except as a traitors and cowards? India's most important need then, as Tilak saw it, was to expel the foreigners and restore Hindustan to Hindu rule, that is re-stablish *Swarajya*.[1]

The most urgent need of his countrymen, as Gokhale saw it, was education: in the techniques of administration, in the rudiments of public health and sanitation, in the skills of advanced technology, in the basic principles of communal harmony and social equality, in the methods of democratic agitation, and as prerequisites for learning all these things, in element reading and writing. Until Indians could learn to subordinate familial, caste, regional, and communal loyalties to the needs of the nation as a whole, to substitute for the ethic of selfishness a standard of selfless national sacrifice, British rule would have to remain as the one force capable of maintaining internal peace throughout the land. If Gokhale's response to British rule, was one of loyal acquiescence based on an overriding faith in the integrity and beneficence of that which was best in the British tradition, it was by no means the supine surrender of a sycophant or a mendicant to bureaucratic oppression. On the contrary, his faith in the ultimate efficacy of his protests against the latter, first of all, led to his choice of a career in public service, and then sustained Gokhale through a lifetime of hopes deferred and apparent failures. The major responsibility of the public-spirited Indian as he understood it was primarily threefold: to present accurately the demands and opinions of Indian society to the government; to interpret correctly the attitudes and actions of the government to the people and to place before the bar of British public and official judgment those arbitrary and inequitable practices of the government of India, which he considered patently "un-British" in the highest sense, and therefore, in need of rectification. As editor of the *Poona Sarvajanik Sabha Journal*, as Congress leader, as provincial and later supreme legislative councillor, as founder and First Member of the Servants of India Society, as official delegate on several occasions to England, and finally, as a royal commissioner, Gokhale laboured to fulfil this responsibility by petition, public statements, and personal appeals. Gifted, as he was with a unique command of the spoken and written English language, he could most effectively fashion his protests, petitions, and pleas, and by the end of his life the weight of Gokhale's influence upon British official opinion was unsurpassed by that of any Indian. The ethical purity of his life, and his selfless dedication to the social and political regeneration of his country similarly assured him a position of exalted prestige and power in the eyes of many Indians. In his view of human nature, English as well as Indian, Gokhale was an optimist and an idealist. He believed in the progressive perfectibility of all mankind, through the agencies of education, the accurate dissemination of information, and social and material amelioration. In voicing the political demands of his people, he was eminently practical, moderate and invariably constructive. The leadership, he offered India, was evolutionary and international in approach and aspiration. He refused to concede any fundamental antipathy existing at the root of the relationship between England and India, stressing rather the interdependent and harmonious aspects of their cultures and mutual goals. In his own life he had learned to feel at home in both worlds, West and East, and in the lives and labours of such Englishmen as Hume, Wedderburn, Ripon, and Morley in whom he recognized a similar capacity for bridging gaps of geography and culture. Was it not possible then for most

Englishmen and Indians to rise to a level of similar understanding and respond to a similar sense of identification? The answer provided by every phase of Gokhale's life and work is emphatically given in the affirmative. Though he often agitated for seemingly petty reforms, Gokhale's labours when viewed in the perspective of his lifetime may be seen as the patient and unremitting struggle to enshrine equality of opportunity and treatment as the principle governing relations between England and India, Englishmen and Indians, and all peoples within India itself and within the empire at large.

Tilak, on the other hand, was less concerned with equality than liberty. He shared neither Gokhale's aspirations nor his evolutionary inclination. He saw the moat rather than the bridge between his world and that of the West. Where Gokhale was syncretic, Tilak was chauvinistic. Instead of international harmony, he preached the national revolution. His tactics were to agitate and to organize among the masses, to voice the inchoate frustrations and discontent of the downtrodden, and to depict the scapegoat foreigner as the single simple cause of their multiple miseries. He did not openly advocate the obvious panacea of freedom, however, either from press or public platforms, since he would then have been confronted with the unpleasant alternatives of execution for treason, or certain destruction, by raising the banner of revolt and pitting whatever forces he might muster against the power of the British military. Tilak was far too practical a man voluntarily to court martyrdom or self-destruction. He rallied his forces by devious means, and directed them in techniques other than the frontal assault. He adhered to no dogmatic revolutionary theory, and he outlined no long-range programme of action or social reorganization. His ultimate goal was independent India; his immediate goal to secure the reins of political power. He was neither squeamish nor doctrinaire about the methods he employed, so long as they helped further his ends. He saw no inherent contradiction in providing ethical, philosophical justification for political assassination, racial and religious antipathy, or the use of duplicity on the one hand; while avowing his loyalty to British rule and promising to cooperate with the government on the other. In rallying support he did not scruple against appealing to prejudice or mass anxiety, and he did not succumb to the distraction of concerning himself with the aftermath of his tactics. He stimulated the revival of Hindu religious consciousness through the *Ganapati* festivals and similar movements with scant apprehension about their impact on the Muslim community. He stirred Maharashtrian regional pride through the Shivaji festivals and *Kesari* editorials, but did not look to the day when militant regionalism might present a challenge or prove a hindrance to the growth of national unity. He attacked scientific innovations and social reforms as the handmaids of a foreign ideology and foreign religion, thereby strengthening the superstitions, irrational apprehensions, and reactionary prejudices of broad segments of Indian society, providing, many of his less intelligent and enlightened followers with powerful arguments against the introduction of progressive measures so vital for India's development. While Tilak himself may sincerely have believed in the beneficence of the many causes he so ably popularized, at times he appears to have been motivated less by his own faith in the inherent worth of a particular cause by the belief that championing it would prove most expedient in winning him the support of the majority of ideals of fellow countrymen. Conversely, while he personally may not have believed that every social reform he condemned was in itself harmful, or unnecessary, he appears to have been supremely aware of the fact that a potent method of achieving swift popularity was by criticizing unpopular innovations.

The ultimate explanation for the differing responses of Tilak and Gokhale to British rule must remain shrouded in the hidden wellsprings of their personalities and those unrecorded potent influences of heredity and early environment. Admittedly, the fact that Tilak was a Brahman helps explain the virulence of his reaction to the inroads of a foreign faith in his nation at the expense of his own religion. But Gokhale and Ranade were also Brahmans. Like Tilak, they too were of the *Chitpavan* community, which might otherwise be considered a significant reason for Tilak's disaffection from British rule since the *Chitpavans* had been temporal as well as spiritual leaders in Maharashtra before their conquest by the British. Similarly, were it not for the fact that both Agarkar and Gokhale had joined Fergusson College at an early age, belonging to the Deccan Education Society as well, Tilak's membership in such autonomous educational institutions might in itself be looked upon as an evidence of his early revolutionary ardor. No such temptingly simple explanations, however, are possible. Yet, if the mysteries of individuality doom to failure, the search for definitive causes of the initial differences of their responses, to British rule, the reactions of British opinion to these responses, were surely factors of vital importance in formulating the later attitudes of each of them towards the British government of India.

In one sense Tilak's life may be seen as a protracted and losing battle against the machinery of British justice. For him the court of law almost invariably proved the first stop on the road to prison. His most intimate and extensive contact with Western thought and Englishmen came from the Indian Penal Code, trial procedure, and British judges, magistrates, prosecutors, and police officers, who with the aid of their Indian counterparts repeatedly compelled him to endure the hardships and humiliations of physical restraint. Though he invariably pleaded innocent when tried, openly apologizing as he did in the Barve case, or else denying any intention of preaching sedition or racial hatred as he did in later trials, most verdicts nonetheless were handed down heavily against him. Surely he soon came to feel that no matter what he said or did, official opinion had branded him a sedition monger once for all, and this must have helped convince him that until India won *swarajya*, though others might profit from liberal changes in British rule, he and his party could hope for little beyond strict surveillance and continued harassment.

Gokhale, on the other hand, was brought into warm personal contact with the leaders of English liberalism at the age of thirty when he first visited England, and thereafter could never limit his appraisal of Englishmen, and the potential which British rule ultimately offered him to the worst specimens in the service of England in India, or the meanest examples of their behaviour. He had access to rooms in British society which were for ever closed to Tilak, just as those cells of foreign rule so long inhabited by Tilak were mercifully not included in Gokhale's experience. Little wonder then if with such different portraits of the Western world, and its representatives indelibly impressed upon the minds of Tilak and Gokhale they each staunchly adhered to their diverging views of how their nation's problems could best be solved.

In the fullness of time, Gokhale felt, as England came to recognize the good faith and capacity of more and more Indians to guide their own people along the path of social progress and reform, she would rely ever more readily upon them to assume control in the land of their birth. Ultimately India would evolve into a dominion like Canada, and freely enjoy the fruits of her long apprenticeship. Having learned step by step the art of self-government, with a populace trained to understand the responsibilities as well as the privileges of democracy, India's bloodless transition from a caste and priest-ridden society of many kingdoms to a modern secular national state would have been completed. This was Gokhale's dream for his land, and though it had all the virtues of a scholar's blueprint for the refashioning of a body politic, it was drawn without reckoning on the unknown quantities of human passions, prejudices, and impatience. These latter elements were the very ingredients, most adroitly utilized by Tilak, who refused to concede that India's body politic needed the plastic surgery of Western institutions grafted upon it. To Tilak, the difference between English and Indian society was one of kind, not of degree, and he mocked the callow rashness of those who ever quick to claim that what was newer was necessarily better. His dream was not an India made in its foreign master's single but one restored to the glory of its own true Self. The quicker the British left, the happier he and his land would be. There could be no salvation for India in self-deception of constitutional co-operation. Better to rely on the *yoga* of boycott. There was no profit for Indians in the prosperity of Lancashire. Let the *videshi* burn, and spread the sale of *swadeshi* cloth instead. Why trouble India's youth with the study of Western culture in a language their ancestors never spoke? National education in the dialects of each region would teach them all they needed to know, and instill in their hearts the pride and self-confidence of men bequeathing a priceless heritage of their own civilization. Of what value was an extra seat, or for that matter an extra hundred seats, in the Council chamber of a foreign government? The birthright of every Indian was the glory of *swarajya*. These were Tilak's demands, and to popular ear that which Gokhale asked for sounded dim, distant, and drab by comparison.

It would be difficult to imagine India today robbed of the legacy of either Tilak or Gokhale. They both set a standard of service in public life, of labour in the national cause, which has rarely been matched, and continues to inspire the leaders of the Republic of India at present, and countless numbers among the more humble citizens of the world's most populous democracy. In many respects, Indian society has evolved and will continue to evolve along lines of an uneasy compromise between the dreams of each of them. Choosing independence as Tilak would have done, the Republic of India has, in Gokhale fashion retained strong ties of fraternity with England and the sterling bloc through her membership in the commonwealth. Similarly, within the nation as well the progressive Westernization along liberal lines of constitutional development may be pointed to as part of the living Gokhale tradition; while militancy, resurgent Hinduism, regional and communal sensitivity, caste consciousness, and social conservatism, can be seen as something of the heritage of Tilak. It is beyond the range of this study to consider these contemporary aspects of the Tilak and Gokhale mainstreams in any detail, and it must also be remembered, of course, that some four decades have elapsed since the death of both these great makers of modern India. But just as Tilak and Gokhale were not the first to plunge into their mainstreams of revolution and reform, neither were they the last carriers of these mighty currents wending across the intellectual plain of India's recent history, and fertilizing its rich soil with the inspiration of their thought and the results of their action. The channels cut by each have gone deep into the soil of Indian life, as if they were tenuously joined. This is due to the broad power of Gandhi's remarkable syncretic capacity.

Let us see what was the impression on Gandhiji of Tilak and Gokhale when he met them first in Poona. Gandhiji said, "the Lokamanya (seemed to me) like the ocean. But Gokhale was as the Ganges. One could have a refreshing bath in the Holy river... One could not easily launch forth on the sea, but the Ganges invited one to its bosom. It was a joy to be on it with a boat and an oar."[2]

Gandhi appeared to be annoyed with the writer who wrote him an anonymous letter in which he admired him for taking a cause that was dearest to the Lokamanya's heart; and advised Gandhi that his (Tilak's) spirit was residing in him (Gandhi). In reply to this letter, he wrote: "I cannot claim the honour of being a follower of the late Lokamanya. I admire him like millions of his countrymen for his indomitable will, his vast learning, his love of country, and above all, the purity of his private life and great sacrifice. Of all the men of modern times, he captivated most the imagination of his people. He breathed into us the spirit of *Swaraj*. No one perhaps realized the evil of the existing system of Government as Tilak did. And in all humility I claim to deliver his message to the country as truly as the best of his disciples. But I am conscious that my method is not Tilak's method."[3]

Gandhi went on to add: "I can only hope, that when the final test comes, the country will be proved to have assimilated the method of non-violence, non-cooperation. Nor am I unaware of my other limitations. I can lay no claim to scholarship. I have not his powers of organization, I have no compact disciplined party to lead, and having been in exile for twenty-three years, I cannot claim the experience that the Lokamanya had of India. Two things we had in common to the fullest measure love of country and steady pursuit of *Swaraj*."[4]

This puts into clear relief the difference between and the common foundation of the two leaders. In the two great leaders certainly the love of the country and steady pursuit of the goal of self-independence for Motherland was common. It was, however, modest on the part of Gandhi to have said that he did not have the scholarship or the potentiality of organization or acumen to lead a disciplined party. All of us know that he had all these qualities in plenty.

Theodore L. Shay had described the aspect of the love of the country common to both the Lokamanya and the Mahatma in the following words: "The first such principle was love of country. Tilak had always been a nationalist first. To him India was the Mother, the past, the present and the promise of the future, the image for which he demanded the nation's sacrifice and for which he sacrifices himself. Humanitarian principles often motivated Gandhiji's actions, but he recognized that what he did for humanity was of value to the extent that he acted for India, for India was the 'action-environment' in which the universality of his faith and his principles could be demonstrated and proved. Because of this he, too, became a great and devoted son of the Mother (land)."[5]

About *Swaraj* being a common denominator of two leaders, it can be said that Tilak (and Nationalists) first envisaged *Swaraj*. The concept of *Swaraj* as was used by the Lokamanya, could not have been derived from the Western philosophy; but it was in the classical value system. That is what the Lokamanya considered his birth-right and the embodiment of the traditional value of *Bharat Dharma. Swaraj* was political ideal that could be called to have been derived from the light of the Indian civilization. In the words of Aurobindo Ghosh: "God has sent us into the world to fulfil Him by fulfilling ourselves in our individual life, in the family, in the community, in the nation, in humanity."[6]

Gandhiji's independence movement was guided by his great philosophy of politics. His concept of the purpose of struggle and fulfilment of the promise made by the Charter of 1836 and Declaration of Queen Victoria in 1857—the entire meaning was conveyed by the Raj which was to belong to all the people of India—the *Swaraj* of an awakened nation.

After having focused our attention of the common things between these two leaders (Tilak and Gandhi), let us discuss the differences in their approach. The first difference was that Tilak's principle was based on political realism. Gandhi's insistence was on ethical consistency. The second difference between the two leaders could be found in Tilak's conservative political expectations and Gandhiji's initial enthusiastic expectations. While Tilak's cry was that *Swaraj* was his birth-right and he would have it; Gandhiji's initial cry was '*Swaraj* in one year'. This captivated the public imagination. The third difference between the two leaders could be traced to Tilak's militant realism and Gandhi's idealist philosophy. In his own way Tilak was a great idealist for he led in the development of idealist philosophy of independence movement leading to the *Swaraj* for his nation. At the same time Tilak is characteristically thought of as one of India's greatest sons steeped in the past Indian tradition. Gandhi, on the other hand, was an idealist and his idealism was more influenced by Western philosophical concept borrowed from man like Tolstoy, Ruskin, Thoreau, and by the Indian heritage of Jain and Buddhist traditions of India's past political history.

To Tilak, *Swaraj* was completely self-justifying goal; and he constantly recommended to the nation that there was nothing which was not dependent upon *Swaraj*. To him it was the objective to be achieved and he did not bother any great deal about the means to fulfil this objective. Gandhi appeared on the other hand to have some moral justification for the initiation for the non-cooperation and non-civil disobedience but also to devote himself to idealistic means constantly denying on utility of the violence not only on the grounds of its efficiency but also on the ground of moral indefensibility.

Tilak sternly maintained that British Imperial Rule in India was itself immoral and no other justification was needed to battle with the bureaucracy. Gandhi while fighting for *Swaraj* as ultimate goal, nevertheless sought an immediate justification for his campaign and above all stressed the role of pure means to achievement. In 1920, it was the issue of Khilafat and Punjab atrocities which provided him with the moral justification. Gandhi in short, never wavered from *Swaraj* as an ultimate moral reason for political struggle.

Tilak and Gandhi taught the classical message of perfecting the human-self and dedicated themselves to the highest aspiration of truthful living and strove towards achieving *Swadharma*. Self-reliance was the key-note of both the leaders. Tilak wanted to have masses with him but could never manage to achieve this goal. Gandhi's voice reached everyone. He became the man of the masses. Though he spoke softly, his voice had an electrifying effect.

After Tilak, Gandhiji wrote of him, "No man preached the gospel of *Swaraj* with the consistency and the insistence of the Lokamanya. His countryman, therefore, implicitly believed in him. His courage never failed him. His optimism was irrepressible. The Lokamanya had hoped to see *Swaraj* fully established during his lifetime. If he failed, that was not his fault. He certainly brought it nearer by many a year. It is for us who remain behind, to put forth redoubled effort to make it a reality in the shortest possible time. For us, he will go to the generations yet unborn as a maker of modern India. They will revere his memory as of a man who lived for them and died for them."[7]

At the time of the unveiling of the portrait of Tilak at India House, London, Jawaharlal Nehru said: "I have no doubt that in Indian history, Lokamanya Tilak will be revered as the Father of the Indian Revolution for the way in which he built it, prepared people for it and when his strength failed, handed down the torch to Mahatma Gandhi."[8]

Gokhale was a professor-politician with great qualities of head and heart. His simplicity of life was proverbial, his speeches whether in the Imperial Council or outside were very effective. He used to speak chaste English and would attract the attention of both the English and the Indians.

Lord Curzon who himself was a very capable Governor General, used to work eighteen hours, and there was nothing conceivable that he did not have in his mind about the welfare of Indian polity, economy and the society. However, his capabilities eventually made him conceited, and he would not consider any Indian politician worth the name. To begin with, he had also many differences of opinion with Gokhale. Being a conservative Governor General he doubted the capability of Gokhale. But when the clouds were lifted and he had left the country, he spoke about Gokhale as we have already seen as under: "Mr. Gokhale was a member of my Legislative Council during a period of, I suppose, five or six years. During that time he was, I think, I may almost say, in invariable opposition to the Government. He was, if I may describe him, the leader of the Opposition in the Imperial Legislative Council over which I presided. In that capacity I often had to suffer from the weight of Mr. Gokhale's blows, but I should like to say this, that I have never met a man of any nationality more gifted with what one could describe in this country as Parliamentary capacities, than was Mr. Gokhale. I truly believe.... (he) would have attained a position of distinction in any parliament in the world."[9]

It is also well-known that Gokhale could not be purchased by any award or title conferred or recommended by the Governor General or approved by His Majesty. For instance, Lord Hardinge, the Viceroy of India opened the meeting of the Imperial Legislative Council held on February 23, with appraisal of Gokhale's qualities. Talking of his personal relations with Gokhale, Hardinge said: "I have always regarded him not merely as an important member of my Council but also as a friend. On more than one occasion, he has given me advice which I found to be both sound and useful and I may mention that in the South Africa Immigration question he rendered me most loyal and helpful assistance. It was only six months ago that I recommended to His Majesty the King Emperor, the appointment of Mr. Gokhale as Knight Commander of the Indian Empire as a mark of recognition of his valuable services, but Mr. Gokhale with that simplicity of his nature which characterized him, gratefully acknowledged the intention but asked to remain as he was."[10]

Sir Valentine Chirol wrote about Gokhale with reference to his association in the Royal Commission on 'Higher Service'.

"Mr. Gokhale who amongst all the Indians I have known seemed to me to combine the finest qualities of the Eastern Civilization from which he sprang and of the Western Civilization of which he had assimilated the best elements. I already knew and admired him as the courageous founder of the Servants of India Society for the promotion of high ideals of social service to which he devoted a life of strenuous endeavour and ascetic self-denial. If he was an ardent Indian patriot who claimed the release of his country from the leading strings of bureaucratic government, none acknowledged more fully and gratefully all that India owed to the fine example of the integrity and intelligence and industry which the European members of the public service had set before his people and he never hesitated to impress upon the Western educated youth of India that they must not only acquire the knowledge which British rule had opened up to them in modern schools and colleges, but above all emulate the qualities of character to which Britain owed her freedom and her greatness. He was not only a master of the English language and an admirable speaker, but he had the gift of accurate and lucid statement and of logical reasoning which the ablest Indians often lack; and though Curzon was apt to regard his political independence as tainted with sedition, he was almost the only Indian whom that masterful Viceroy never ventured to treat as a negligible quantity in Council. In the intimacy which grew up between us during the three years we worked together on the Royal Commission, I learnt to entertain a deep and sincere affection for a man who could always understand the Englishman's view, even when he could least share it and knew at the same time how to interpret with firmness and courtesy the very different and often antagonistic standpoint of the Indian. To him I owe a clearer insight than I had ever pined before into the rational and legitimatc political aspirations of his fellow countrymen, deriving straight from the Western education we have given them and to him also a deeper understanding of the society brought up as a high caste Chitpavan Brahman. For if he had leant to measure and deplore its shortcomings in the light of all the best that the West could teach him, he had too much self-respect to depreciate lightly the ancient civilization in which India had lived and moved and had her being from the very dawn of history."[11]

The editor of *The Statesman* who used to carry on the propaganda of the lobby of Anglo-Indians in India wrote about Gokhale on 15 February, 1915: "Mr. Gokhale was the greatest leader that India had ever produced, perhaps her greatest man."[12]

Few days later at a memorial meeting in London, a member of India Council referred to Gokhale as the greatest Indian of his time. Mrs. Annie Besant who was a leader of Home Rule League, the founder of Central Hindu College, Banaras and a member of a Theosophical Society pleaded with Gokhale in 1914, "You know that India cannot spare you and a month or two may mean years of work."[13]

Rabindranath Tagore in December 1913 wrote to Gokhale, "You must remember that for a man like you to live is in itself a service to your country for your life is not merely useful, it is a light to others."[14]

Mahatma Gandhi had always considered Gokhale as his political *guru*; and his praise for Gokhale was unparalleled. He quoted a

Sloka from the *Bhagwad Gita* (9-27) meaning in English: "Whatever you do, whatever you eat, whatever you offer as a sacrifice of gift, whatever austerity you performed, Oh Kaunteya dedicate it all to me."[15] After having quoted this *sloka*, Mahatma Gandhi said, "It seems that Mahatma Gokhale functioned as the words addressed by Krishna to Arjuna had been addressed to him by India the mother of us all and had been made by him the guiding principle of his life. For it will be readily admitted that whatever he did, whatever he enjoyed, whatever he sacrificed, whatever he gave in charity, whatever austerities he performed (for the sake of achieving self-independence for his country), he dedicated them all to his motherland."[16]

Gandhi had an unparalleled respect for Gokhale: "It was different with Gokhale, I cannot say why? I met him at his quarters on the college ground. It was like meeting an old friend, or better still a mother after a long separation. His gentle face put me at ease in a moment. His minute inquiries about myself and my doings in South Africa at once enshrined him in my heart. And as I parted from him, I said to myself, you are my man and from that moment Gokhale never lost sight of me. In 1901 on my second return from South Africa, we came closer still. He simply took me in hand, and began to fashion me. He was concerned about how I spoke, dressed, walked and ate. My mother was not more solicitous about me than Gokhale. There was, so far as I am aware, no reserve between us. It was really a case of love at first sight, and it stood the severest strain in 1913. He seemed to me all I wanted as a political worker—pure as crystal, gentle as a lamb, brave as a lion, and chivalrous to a fault. It does not matter to me that he may not have been any of these things. It was enough for me that I could discover no fault in him to cavil at. He was and remains for me the most perfect man on the political field."[17]

Gandhi has left a very illustrative pen picture of Gokhale which explains what Gokhale was in the freedom of India. He observed: "To see Gokhale at work was as much a joy as an education. He never wasted a minute. His private relations and friendships were all for public good. All his talks had reference only to the good of the country and were absolutely free from any trace of untruth on insincerity. India's poverty and subjection were matters of constant and intense concern to him. Various people sought to interest him in different things. But he gave everyone of them the same reply: 'You do the thing yourself. Let me do my own work. What I want is freedom for my country. After that is won, we can think of other things. Today that one thing is enough to engage all my time and energy'."[18]

Gokhale always stood for communal harmony in the country. We have already discussed how cheerfully he was received by the students of Mohammadan-Anglo Oriental College at Aligarh when he came to this Institution. The students unhorsed the *baggi*, and drove him themselves in place of the horses and said, 'Gokhale Zindabad'.

On the same issue Mahatma Gandhi has written that Gokhale had as much pride in Muslims as the Hindus. In fact his standpoint on the Hindu-Muslim relation was purely religious. Gandhi observed: "Once a Hindu monk came to him in order to prevail upon him to grant an inferior status to the Mussalmans and to secure an advantage for the Hindus. But Gokhale would not listen to him. The monk complained that the great leader did not take pride in Hinduism. At this Gokhale frowned and said, 'If Hinduism consists in doing what you say, I am not a Hindu. Please, therefore, leave me.' And the so-called monk left the man who was a real *Sannyasi*."[19]

Gokhale treated Gandhi just as his own child. There are several themes that Gandhi has elaborated which indicate that it was so. For instance, he said to him: "On board the same steamer we were engaged in a hot discussion in connection with our dear Motherland, and he was mapping out for me, as a father would for his child, a programme that I was to follow in India if I ever happened to see the Motherland again. In that connection he said: "We in India lack character, we need religious zeal in the political field." One of his missions in life, I think, was to inculcate the lesson that whatever we do, we should do with zeal and thoroughness. Whatever he did, he did with a religious passion; that was the secret of his success. He did not wear his religion on his sleeves; he lived it. Whatever he touched, he purified, wherever he went, he created an atmosphere around him which was fragrant."[20]

Similarly, Gokhale taught Gandhi not only the love of the country and the glorification of the language, but also spiritualization of its political life and its institution. Gandhi has said: "Gokhale taught me that the dream of every Indian who claims to love his country, should be not to glorify the country in language but to spiritualize its political life and institutions. He inspired my life and is still inspiring it in that I wish to purify myself and spiritualize myself. I have dedicated myself to that ideal. I may fail, and to the extent I fail, I am an unworthy disciple of my master."[21]

It is well-known that even though a Moderate and having a faith and trust in the British democracy and ideal of equality and fraternity, Gokhale always acted in the Imperial Council as a leader of opposition. Though, he himself lived in poverty and austerity, he did everything for the service of the country without any expectation of praise or reward from anyone. For instance, M.K. Gandhi has said about him: "There is no one who can tell you as much about Mr. Gokhale as I can, about his life in the political arena of India. He it is who gave twenty years of his life to the cause of education for a mere pittance. Even today Mr. Gokhale lives in poverty although he can command riches. Hundreds of pounds are always at his disposal whenever he wants them for public institutions. A Viceroy of India carried the burden of Empire on his shoulders for five years (unless he was a Lord Curzon, who held Office for seven), and even then had a train of workers to assist him, but here is a distinguished countrymen of mine carrying the burden of Empire on his shoulders unaided and unassisted and undecorated. True, he has won the C.I.E., but in my opinion he is worth a much better decoration. The decoration that Mr. Gokhale loves best is the love of his countrymen, and the approval of his own conscience. To those Indians who are educated on Western lines, he has given a lesson in humility and gentleness."[22]

Gokhale always told his friends and disciples not to waste any time in writing his biographies or trying to glorify him. What he wanted was that instead of erecting a memorial in his honour, people should live a simple life and devote their time to the service of the nation.

Gandhi has said about this aspect: "Now about the portrait, Gokhale was not hungry for fame or honour; indeed it is known that he did not like to receive honours. Many a time when honour was bestowed on him in person he had his eyes turned to the ground. It is certainly not true that Gokhale's soul would enjoy peace by the unveiling of a portrait of his. While on his deathbed, the Mahatma had declared his ideal. He had said that his soul would not enjoy peace if after his death his biography was written, or if a memorial was raised to him, or if meetings were held to express sorrow at his passing away from this world. His only desire was that the whole of India should lead the life he had led and that the Servants of India Society founded by him progressed and prospered in its mission of service to the nation. Only those who accept the spirit of this last will and statement of the departed soul have the right to have a portrait of Gokhale and to get it unveiled."[23]

In addition to the communal harmony his mind was engaged to find out the ways of uplifting the down-trodden and the untouchables. Gandhi has said of him: "Between the Hindu and the Mussalman Gokhale did make any differences whatsoever. In his eyes everyone was equal and he had the same love for all. He gave way to anger sometimes, but his anger had in all cases to do with the good to the country. Besides, his anger had a benevolent effect on the opposite party concerned. His indignation was so disinterested that many Europeans who at first disliked him later became his close friends.

"The question of uplifting the 'untouchable' was uppermost in the mind of Gokhale and he initiated and carried on various activities for their welfare. If anyone dared to criticize him for this, he frankly told him that we did not commit sin by touching them but by refusing to touch them."[24]

Mahatma Gandhi has emphasized that Gokhale used to work in whatever capacity he did in the spirit of a devotee with courage, truthfulness, patience, straightforwardness and perseverance. That is to say that what Gokhale did in public life, he meant it. He always emphasized the public life must be spiritualized. "If therefore we would learn a lesson from the life of this great patriot we should follow his method of working in the spirit of a devotee. Everyone of us cannot become a member of the Supreme Legislature and members of that Legislature are not always seen in the ranks of the servants of the nation. Everyone cannot serve on the Public Service Commission and men designated as its members are not always found rendering service to the country. We cannot all acquire learning like him and learned men do not always serve the people. But we can all cultivate virtues like courage, truthfulness, patience, humility, a sense of justice, straightforwardness and perseverance and dedicate them to the nation. This is the spirit of a devotee. This is what Gokhale meant when he spoke of 'public life being spiritualized'. All who conduct themselves in such a spirit of dedication will always see their way clear before them and claim a share in legacy which Gokhale has left for us all. Such devoted workers will be endowed with all such gifts as they need, as the Lord has promised and Gokhale's life is an illustration of that promise having been abundantly fulfilled."[25]

Gandhi's respect and devotion for Gokhale was that of a disciple for a *Guru*. It gave him the greatest pleasure whenever he personally served Gokhale in any capacity whatsoever. A very interesting type of service Gandhi did for Gokhale, and believed that he got the greatest certificate of his life, was to iron the scarf given to Gokhale by his *guru* M.G. Ranade. When Gokhale praised him as a good washerman, Gandhi said that it was the greatest and the most valuable certificate by him.

When Gokhale died, Gandhi took a vow not to put on any chappal for the whole year. That was the respect in which he held his 'political *guru*'. He also said that in politics he wanted to have a pilot who could help him going straight without any difficulty and he found one in Gokhale. But alas after his death he had to depend on his own resources.

What Pandit Motilal Nehru said illustrates the personality and character of Gopal Krishna Gokhale. He said, "He was a noble soul fired by a patriotism that was all-consuming. A born leader of man, he never aspired to anything but to be the humblest servant of the motherland in whose services he brought such devotion into play that it is now a matter of history. He lived up to the very high ideal which he set before himself and his countrymen and cannot better than to describe that ideal in his own inimitable language. In one of his speeches he said, 'Public life must be spiritualized. Love of country must so fill the heart that all else shall appear as of little moment by its side. A fervent patriotism which rejoices at every opportunity of sacrifices for the motherland, a dauntless heart which refuses to be turned back from its object by difficulty or danger, a deep faith in the purpose of providence that nothing can shake, equipped with these the worker must start on his mission and reverently seek the joy which comes of spending oneself in the service of the motherland.' These were the noble words he uttered and that was the ideal he strictly followed in his life and true to his words, he literally, actually spent himself in the service of the motherland."[26]

Similarly, Pandit Madan Mohan Malviya, the founder of Banaras Hindu University, has said of him: "We have had many illustrious men during the last hundred years and I hope we shall have many more in the coming years. There will be men probably with equal intellectual qualifications, with equally earnest patriotism, but a combination of the qualities which made Mr. Gokhale dear to the whole country is not easily to be looked for."[27]

Sir Sivaswamy lyer has also given a pen picture of Gokhale when he said, "A life like Gokhale's is full of lessons to all and to every public worker, every citizen. The pains that Mr. Gokhale took to master his subjects, his culture, his wide outlook, his sound judgement, his sweet reasonableness and his spirit of compromise, his avoidance of personal questions, his self-denial, his unwavering determination to do the right and his tenacity of purpose are all worthy of the highest imitation. It may not be given to all to possess Mr. Gokhale's abilities or constructive statesmanship, but it is open to everyone to work for the public good in the spirit which animated him and with his high ideals which guided him."[28]

In his autobiography Jawaharlal Nehru has written that he was attracted by the Servants of India Society founded by Gokhale. Even though he could not become a member of the Servants of India Society, yet was greatly impressed by the idea of whole time public service on the lines of Gokhale's personal example. He has described Gokhale as: "high-strung, full of earnestness and a nerve of energy and one of the few persons present who took politics and public affairs seriously and felt deeply about them."[29]

Aga Khan who was the founder of Muslim League and running parallel institution in London with Ali Imam as his co-worker to the British Committee of Indian National Congress, said that as a person Gokhale was a great gentleman: "his power of winning love and affection. We often regretted as we sat by him that there was no counting house in the universe where we could go and transfer a few years of our healthy life to the account of Gopal Krishna Gokhale."[30]

Mohammad Ali Jinnah has perhaps paid the greatest homage to Gokhale when he said that it was his "one ambition to become Muslim Gokhale."[31]

Gokhale on his own part had always believed that Gandhi was the most promising political leader to work in India. While addressing a meeting in Albert Hall in Calcutta as early as on June 19,1902 Gokhale said that Gandhi was "made of the stuff of which heroes were made." He had proved that the fiercest opposition could be overcome and the bitterest misunderstanding removed, if only they were true to themselves and worked in a correct, selfless, straightforward manner, and did not return insult for insult, abuse for abuse. "if Mr. Gandhi settled in this country," continued Gokhale, "it was the duty of all earnest workers to place him where he deserved to be at their head.[32]

Similarly, after having gone to South Africa to help Gandhi in his struggle for the Indians abroad, when Gokhale returned and was told by one of his friends that some people particularly Pherozshah Mehta (the lion of Bombay) did not think highly of his work in assisting Gandhi, Gokhale was very unhappy. He observed: "Start a dignified agitation if you have the stuff in you; go about the country, make the kind of sacrifices that Mr. Gandhi and others have made, and then insist upon free immigration into South Africa. It is all very well to sit at home and criticize men like Mr. Gandhi. God knows that most of us are poor enough clay, and when once in a way a man rises amongst us, here we are sitting quiet at home and criticizing him and tearing him to pieces in the manner that some of us are doing."[33]

All this shows that Gopal Krishna Gokhale not only had the capability of working as a perfect spiritualized politician of the country but also had the power of discerning the capability of a young promising man. It is always easy to say well about a big man. But to foresee someone was very promising and then train and encourage him/her to become one as such was a rare quality that not many people can be supposed to possess. It is no exaggeration to say that even if one is not prepared to recognise the greatness of Gokhale for his own work (which as a matter of fact must be done), at least honest persons would have to admit that the very fact of grooming Gandhi to attain the status that he reached was the greatest contribution of Gokhale. A veteran socialist leader and a former High Commissioner at London, Nana Sahib Gore, told this author in Pune that Gokhale died as a frustrated man. In fact frustration is not the word for him. Happy are those who could reach a status of life which is hardly one hundredth part of the one which Gokhale reached.

Tilak was indeed a great politician, a great Builder of Modern India, if a builder could anyone be, who through his own way tried to achieve *Swaraj* by the techniques of Boycott, National Education and *Swadeshi*. But if these were not combined with sweet reasonableness of Gokhale who believed in the removal of obsolete traditions, Bigotry, untouchability and all such evils that had crept up in the Indian society, economy and polity, nothing worthwhile could have been achieved. It has been aptly pointed out by Professor S. Nurul Hasan, a scholar of greater eminence, that it is the electic approach of Gokhale and Tilak which was responsible for whatever social, political and economic reconstruction we were able to achieve in our country.

REFERENCES

1. Wolpert Stanley, *Tilak and Gokhale* (Berkeley: University of California Press), 1962, p. 298.
2. Gandhi, M.K., *Gokhale My Political Guru, op. cit.*, p. 9.
3. *Ibid.*, pp. 52-53.
4. *Ibid.*, p. 53.
5. Shay, Theodore, *The Legacy of Lokmanya, op. cit.*, pp. 156-57.

6. Ghose, Aurobindo, *Speeches, op. cit.*, pp. 85-86.
7. Parvate, T.V., *Gopal Krishna Gokhale, op. cit.*, p. 10.
8. *Ibid.*, p. 539.
9. *Debate on Indian Affairs*, House of Lord Session, 1914-16, 5 & 6 (London: George V.), 1916, p. 114.
10. Parvate, T.V., *Gopal Krishna Gokhale, op. cit.*, p. 453.
11. *Ibid.*, pp. 453-54.
12. *Statesman*, 21 February, 1915.
13. *Annie Besant to Gokhale*, 12 May 1914 (Gokhale Papers).
14. *R. Tagore to Gokhale*, 9 December 1913 (Gokhale Papers).
15. Gandhi, M.K., *Gokhale My Political Guru, op. cit.*, p. 35.
16. *Ibid.*, p. 36.
17. *Ibid.*, p. 55.
18. *Ibid.*, p.11.
19. *Ibid.*, p. 41.
20. *Ibid.*, pp. 60-61.
21. *Ibid.*, p. 59.
22. *Ibid.*, p. 58.
23. *Ibid.*, pp. 63-64.
24. *Ibid.*, pp. 64-65.
25. *Ibid.*, pp. 42-43
26. Parvate, T.V., *Gopal Krishna Gokhale, op. cit.*, pp. 446-47.
27. *Ibid.*, p. 446.
28. *Ibid.*
29. *Ibid.*, p. 430.
30. *Ibid.*, p. 437.
31. *Ibid.*, p. 426.
32. *Indian Mirror*, 26 January, 1902.
33. *Karve and Ambedkar*, Vol. II, *op. cit.*, p. 463.

BIBLIOGRAPHY

Ambirajan, S., *Political Economy and Monetary Management in India, 1766-1914* (Madras: Affiliated East West Press), 1984.

Athalye, D.V., *The Life of Lokmanya Tilak* (Poona: Annasahib Chiploonkar), 1921.

Azad, A.K., *India Wins Freedom* (New York: Longman), 1960.

Banerjea, S.N., *A Nation in Making: Being the Reminisance of Fifty Years* (London: Milford), 1925.

Banerji, A.K. *Aspects of Indo-British Economic Relations, 1858-1898* (Bombay: Oxford University Press), 1982.

Banerji, Arun, *Finances in the Early Raj: Investments and the External Sector* (New Delhi: Sage Publications), 1995.

Black, R.D. *Collison, Economic Thought and the Irish Question, 1817-1870* (Cambridge: Cambridge University Press),1960.

Bapat, S.V. (ed.), *Gleanings from Tilak's Writings and Speeches* (Poona: S.V. Bapat), 1926.

Bapat, S.V. (ed.) *The Reminiscences and the Anecdotes of Lokmanya Tilak*, Vol. II (Poona: S.V. Bapat), 1925.

Blaug, Mark, "Kuhn *versus* Lakatos or Paradigms *versus* Research Programmes in the history of economics" in *Method and Appraisal in Economics*, edited by Spiro J. Latsis (Cambridge: Cambridge University Press), 1976.

Blaug, Mark, *Economic Theory in Retrospect* (Cambridge: Cambridge University Press), 1978.

Bose, S.C., *The Indian Struggle (1920-34)* (Calcutta: Publications for Netaji Publishing Society), 1948.

Cashman, Richard, I., *The Myth of Lokmanya* (Berkeley: University of California Press), 1975.

Central Statistical Organisation, *National Accounts Statistics: Sources and Methods* (New Delhi: Department of Statistics, Ministry of Planning, Government of India), 1989.

Chakarverty, S., "Drain Theory of Dadabhai Naoroji," a paper presented to the Indian Economic Association Conference, December, 1968.

Chandra, Bipan, The Rise and Growth of Economic Nationalism in India, *Economic Policies of Indian National Leadership 1880-1905* (New Delhi: People's Publishing House), 1966.

Charlesworth, Neil, *British Rule and the Indian Economy, 1800-1914* (London: Macmillan), 1982.

Chatterjee, D.K., *C.R. Das and Indian National* (Calcutta: Bhattachariya), 1965.

Chatterjee, R.N., *On Labour Capital* (Calcutta: Chatterjee & Co.), n.d.

Chaudhuri, K.N., "India's International Economy in the Nineteenth Century: An Historical Survey", *Modern Asian Studies*, Vol. 2, No.1 (January), 1968.

Chintamani, C.Y., *Indian Politics Since the Mutiny* (New Delhi: Rupa), 2002.

Chiplunkar, Vishnushastri, *Nibandh Mula* (Poona: S.V. Bapat), 1926.

Chirol, Valentine, *Indian Unrest* (London: Macmillan), 1910.

Coase, R.H., *Essays on Economics and Economists* (Chicago: The University of Chicago Press), 1994.

Clark, Colin, *Conditions of Economic Progress* (London: MacMillan and Co. Ltd.), 1949.

Dantwala, M.L., *Poverty in India, Then and Now, 1870-1970* (Delhi: MacMillan), 1973.

Das, C.R. and Bhagwan Das, *Outline Scheme of Swaraj* (Bombay: Swastik), 1923.

Das, M.N., *Indian National Congress Versus the British*, Vol. 1, *(1885-1918)*, Delhi, 1978.

Dasgupta, Ajit K., *A History of Indian Economic Thought* (London: Routledge), 1993.

Dasgupta, Hemendranath, *Deshbandhu Chittaranjan Das* (New Delhi: Publications Division, Ministry of Information and Broadcasting, Government of India), 1960.

Datta, Bhabatosh, *Indian Economic Thought–Twentieth Century Perspectives* (New Delhi: Tata McGraw Hill Publishing Company Ltd.), 1962.

Datta, Bhabatosh, *The Evolution of Economic Thinking in India (Dr. P.N. Banerjea Memorial Lectures, 1961)* (Calcutta: Federation Hall Society), 1962.

Desai, S.S.M., *Economic History of India* (New Delhi: Himalaya Publishing House), 1990.

Deogirikar, T.R., *Gopal Krishna Gokhale* (New Delhi: Publications Division, Ministry of Information and Broadcasting, Government of India), 1950.

Dimand, Robert W., "I have no Great Faith in Political Arithmetick: Adam Smith and Quantitative Political Economy" in *Measurement, Quantification and Economic Analysis: Numeracy in Economics,* edited by Ingrid H. Rima (London: Routledge), 1995.

Dutt, R. Palme, *India Today* (Delhi: People's Publishing House), 1955.

Dutt, Romesh, *The Economic History of India under the British Rule*, Vols. 1, 2 & 3 (New Delhi: Publications Division, Ministry of Information and Broadcasting, Government of India), 1963.

Dwyer, M.O, *India as I Knew It* (London: Seluryin Blornt), 1935

Gandhi, M.K., *An Autobiography or The Story of My Experiments With Truth* (Ahmedabad: Navajivan Publishing House), 1942.

Gandhi, M.K., *Constructive Programme: Its Meaning ansd Scope* (Ahmedabad: Navajivan Publishing House), 1952.

Gandhi, M.K., *Gokhale–My Political Guru* (Ahmedabad: Navajivan Publishing House), 1952.

Ganguli, B.N., *Dadabhai Naoroji and the Drain Theory* (New York: Asia Publishing House), 1965.

Ganguli, B.N., *Indian Economic Thought: Nineteenth Century Perspectives* (New Delhi: Tata McGraw-Hill Publishing Co. Ltd.), 1978.

Georgescu-Roegen, Nicholas, *Analytical Economics: Issues and Problems* (Cambridge, Massachusetts: Harvard University Press), 1966.

Ghose, Aurobindo, *Bankim-Tilak-Dayananda* (Calcutta: Arya Publishing House), 1940.

Ghose, Aurobindo, *The Foundations of Indian Culture* (New York: The Sri Aurobindo Library), 1953.

Ghose, Aurobindo, *The Ideal of the Karmayogin* (Pondicherry: Sri Aurobindo Ashram), 1950

Gopalakrishnan, P.K., *Development of Economic Ideas in India, 1880-1914* (Gravenhange: Institute of Social Studies), 1954.

Gupta, Ajit Das, *A History of Indian Economic Thought* (Madras: T.R. Publications Private Limited), 1990.

Ingrid H. Rima (ed.), *Measurement, Quantification and Economic Analysis: Numeracy in Economics* (London: Routledge), 1995.

Iyer, C.S. Ranga, *India in the Crucible* (London: Seluryin Blornt), 1928.

Jenk, L.H., British Experience with Foreign Investments," *Journal of Economic History*, 1944.

Jha, Shiva Chandra, *A History of Indian Economic Thought* (Calcutta: Firma K. L. Mukhopadhyay), 1981.

Jog, N.G., *Lokmanya Bal Gangadhar Tilak* (New Delhi: Publications Division, Ministry of Information and Broadcasting, Government of India), 1962.

Karmakar, A.D., *Economic Thought of Modern India* (Dharwar: J.S.S., Institute of Economic Research), 1974.

Karunakaran, K.P., *Indian Politics From Dadabhai Naoroji to Gandhi: A Study of the Political Ideas of Modern India* (New Delhi: Gitanjali Publishing House), 1988.

Kelkar, N.C. *Landmarks in Lokamanya's Life* (Madras: Ganesan & Co.), 1924.

Khan, Sir, Syed Ahmad, *The Complete Collection of Lectures and Speeches* (ed.) by M.I. Gujarati (Lahore: Nawal Kishore), n.d.

Knight, Robert, *India: A Review of England's Financial Relations Therewith* (London: W.J. Johnson), 1968.

Kulkarni, A.V., *Lokmanya Tilak* (Bombay: Inderprakash Steam Press), 1909.

Kurdas, Cigdern, "The Whig Historian on Adam Smith: Paul Samuelson's Canonical Model", *History of Economics Society Bulletin*, Vol. X, No. 1 (Spring), 1988.

Lakatos, Imre, "Falsification and the Methodology of Scientific Research Programmes" in *Criticism and the Growth of Knowledge,* edited by Imre Lakatos and Alan Musgrave (Cambridge: Cambridge University Press), 1970.

Lipton, Michael and Ravallion, Martin, "Poverty and Policy", Policy Research Working Papers, No. WPS 1130 (Washington: The World Bank), 1993.

Loganathan, *A History of Economic Thought* (New Delhi: S. Chand and Company Ltd.), 1987.

Madan, G.R., *Economic Thinking in India* (Madras: S. Chand & Co.), 1982.

Mahajan, O.P., The Drain Theory: Fact and Fiction (IEA), 1968.

Majumdar, Jatindra, Kumar (ed.), *Indian Speeches and Documents on British Rule 1821-1918* (London), 1937.

Masani, R.P., *Builders of Modern India - Dadabhai Naoroji* (New Delhi: Publications Division, Ministry of Information and Broadcasting, Government of India), 1960.

Masani, R.P., *Dadabhai Naoroji: The Grand Old Man of India* (London: George Allen and Unwin Ltd), 1939.

Masani, R.P., *Dadabhai Naoroji* (New Delhi: Publications Division, Ministry of Information and Broadcasting, Government of India), 1960.

Marx Karl and Fredrick Engels, *On Colonialism* (Moscow: Progress Publishers), 1965.

Mill, John Stuart, *Principles of Political Economy*, edited by W.J. Ashley (London: Longmans, Green and Co.), 1909.

Minto, *Many Countries of India, Minto and Morley 1905-1910* (London: Macmillan), 1934.

Morrison, Sir Theodore, *Economic Transition in India* (London: London Press), 1916.

Mukherjee, M., *National Income of India: Trends and Structure* (Calcutta: Statistical Publishing Society), 1969.

Mukerjee, Tapan, "Theory of Economic Drain: Impact of British Rule on the Indian Economy: 1840-1900" in *Economic*

Imperialism: A Book of Readings, edited by K.E. Boulding and Tapan Mukherjee (Ann Arbor: The University of Michigan Press), 1972.

Nabers, Lawrence, 'The Positive and Genetic Approaches' in *The Structure of Economic Science Essays on Methodology*, edited by Sherman Roy Krupp (Englewood Cliffs, N.J.: Prentice-Hall, Inc.), 1966.

Nanda, B.R., *Gokhale* (Delhi: Oxford University Press), 1977.

Nanda, B.R., *Gokhale, Gandhi and the Nehru's Studies in Indian Nationalism* (London: George Allen and Unwin Ltd.), 1990.

Nanda, B.R., *Three Statesmen: Gokhale, Gandhi and Nehru* (Delhi: Oxford University Press), 2004.

Naoroji, Dadabhai, *A Sketch of his Life and Career* (Madras: G. A. Natesan & Co.), 1920.

Naoroji, Dadabhai, *Speeches and Writings of Dadabhai Naoroji* (Madras: G.A. Natesan & Co.), n.d.

Naoroji, Dadabhai, *The Financial Administration of India* (London: W.J. Johnson), 1871.

Naoroji, Dadabhai, *Essays, Speeches, Addresses and Writings* (Bombay: Caxton Printing Works), 1899.

Naoroji, Dadabhai, *Poverty and Un-British Rule in India* (New Delhi: Publications Division, Government of India), 1962.

Naoroji, Dadabhai, *India's Wrongs and Remedy* (Madras: The Commonwealth Office), 1917.

Nehru, Jawaharlal, *Autobiography* (London: The Bodley Head), 1947.

Okakura, *Ideals of the East* (Calcutta: Editions Indian), 1973.

Pal, Bepin Chandra, *His Life and Utterances* (Madras: Ganesan & Co.), 1925.

Pandey, Shridhar, *Economic History of India* (Hindi) (Patna: Motilal Banarsidass), 1991.

Parekh C.L., *Essays, Speeches, Address and Writings* (on Indian Politics) of the Hon'ble Dadabhai Naoroji (Bombay: Asia Publishers), 1887.

Parliamentary Debates (House of Commons), Fourth Series, Vol. XI, 13th April 1893.

Parvate, T.V., *Bal Gangadhar Tilak* (Ahmedabad: Navajivan Publishing House), 1958.

Parvate, T.V., *Gopal Krishna Gokhale* (Ahmedabad: Navajivan Publishing House), 1958.

Patwardhan, R.P. (ed.), *Dadabhai Naoroji Correspondence, Child and Youth Section*, Vol. II, Part I (Bombay: Allied Publishers), 1977.

Paul, R.R., *History of Economic Thought* (New Delhi: Kalyani Publishers), 1979.

Pradhan, G.P. and A.K. Bhagwat, *Lokmanya Tilak: A Biography* (Poona: J.S. Tilak), 1963.

Prasad, R., *At the Feet of Mahatma Gandhi* (Bombay: Asia Publishing House), 1961.

Price Powell, *A History of India* (London: Thomas Nelson and Sons Limited), 1955.

Ranade, Mahadev Govind, *Ranade's Economic Writings,* edited by Bipan Chandra (New Delhi: Gian Publishing House), 1990.

Rao, V.K.R.V., *An Essay on India's National Income, 1925-1929* (London: George Allen and Unwin), 1939.

Rashid, Salim, "Does a Famous Economist Deserve Special Standards? A Critical Note on Adam Smith Scholarship," *History of Economics Society Bulletin*, Vol. XI, No. 2 (Fall), 1989.

Ray, M.N., *India in Transition* (Bombay: Nachiketa), 1971.

Ray, P.C., *Life and Times of C.R. Das* (Calcutta: Orient Books), 1958.

Robinson, Joan, *An Essay on Marxian Economics* (London: Macmillan), 1966.

Rogin, Leo, *The Meaning and Validity of Economic Theory* (New York: Harper and Bros.), 1956.

Ronaldshay, *Earl of the Heart of Aryavarta*: *A Study of the Psychology of Indian Unrest* (London: Constable), 1925.

Saggi, P.D. (ed.), *Life and Work of Lal, Bal and Pal* (New Delhi: Overseas Publishing House), 1962.

Samuelson, Paul, "The Transfer Problem and Transport Costs: The Terms of Trade when Impediments are Absent," *Economic Journal*, Vol. LXII, No. 246 (June), 1952.

Samuelson, Paul, "Out of the Closet: A Program for the Whig History of Economic Science", *History of Economics Society Bulletin*, IKI (Fall), 1987.

Sastri, V.S.S., *Life of Gopal Krishna Gokhale* (Bangalore: Bangalore Printing Co.), 1937.

Schumpeter, J.A., *History of Economic Analysis* (New York: Oxford University Press), 1954.

Scweinitz, Jr. Karl de, *The Rise and Fall of British India: Imperialism as Inequality* (London: Methuen & Co.), 1983.

Selected Essays of Sister Nivedita (Madras: Ganesan & Co.), 1911.

Sen, R.K. and Mandal, S.K., *Ranade's Analysis of India's Population Problem and The Views of Naoroji and Doskar*, I.E.A., 75th Conference Volume, 1992.

Sen, Rathindra Nath, *Life and Times of Deshbandhu Chittranjan Das* (New Delhi: Northern Book Centre), 1989.

Sen, Sunanda, *Colonies and the Empire India, 1890-1914* (Hyderabad: Orient Longman), 1922.

Shanmugasundaram, V., *Indian Economic Thought and Policy* (New Delhi: S. Chand and Company Ltd.), 1981.

Sharma, Jai Narain, *Power, Politics and Corruption: A Gandhian Solution* (New Delhi: Deep and Deep), 2005.

Sharma, Jai Narain, "Gandhi and the Congress Presidents" in Malhotra, S.C. (ed.) *Gandhi and the Indian National Congress* (Chandigarh: Publications Bureau, Panjab University), 1988.

Shay, Theodore, *The Legacy of Lokmanya* (London: Oxford University Press), 1956.

Singh, V.B., *From Naoroji to Nehru* (New Delhi: MacMillan), 1975.

Sitaramayya, Pattabhi, *History of Indian National Congress 1885-1935*, Vol. I (New Delhi: S. Chand & Co.), 1969.

Spear, T.G.P., *India* (London: Seluryin Blornt), 1935.

Speeches and Writings of Gopal Krishna Gokhale (New York: Asia Publishing House), 1966.

Stark, Werner, *The History of Economics in its Relation to Social Development* (London: Kegan Paul, Trench, Trubner & Co.), 1944.

Studenski, Paul, *The Income of Nations* (New York: New York University Press), 1958.

Tilak, B.G., *Gita Rahasya* (Poona: Tilak Brothers), 1925.

Tilak, B.G., *His Writings and Speeches* (Madras: Ganeshan & Co.), 1922.

Tilak, B.G., *Samagra Lokmanya Tilak*, Vol. IV (Pune: Kesari Prakashan), 1974.

Vaswani, T.L., *India in Chains* (Madras: Ganesan & Co.), 1920.

Viner, Jacob, *Studies in the Theory of International Trade* (London: George Allen and Unwin), 1960.

Wolpert Stanley, *Tilak and Gokhale* (Berkeley: University of California Press), 1962.

World Bank, *World Development Report, 1990* (Oxford: Oxford University Press), 1990.

Zachaias, H.C.E., *Renascent India* (London: Allen), 1933.

Zaidi, A.M. and Others, *The Encycolpaedia of Indian National Congress* (New Delhi: S. Chand & Co.), 1980.

Zaidi Moin A., *Dadabhai Naoroji, Speeches and Writings* (New Delhi: Indian Institute of Applied Political Research), Vol. 1, 1985.

Index